RUDOLF STEINER AND THE SCHOOL FOR SPIRITUAL SCIENCE

Rudolf Steiner's rose cross

Rudolf Steiner and the School for Spiritual Science

The Foundation of the "First Class"

Peter Selg

2012
SteinerBooks

SteinerBooks
An Imprint of Anthroposophic Press, Inc.
610 Main St., Great Barrington, MA 01230
www.steinerbooks.org

Copyright © 2012 by Peter Selg. All rights reserved.
No part of this publication may be reproduced, stored in
a retrieval system, or transmitted, in any form or by any
means, electronic, mechanical, photocopying,
recording, or otherwise, without the prior
written permission of the publisher.

Originally published in German as *Rudolf Steiner und die Freie Hochschule
für Geisteswissenschaft. Die Begründung der «Ersten Klasse»*
Published by Verlag des Ita Wegman Instituts 2008.
Translated by Margot M. Saar

Library of Congress Cataloging-in-Publication Data

Selg, Peter, 1963–
 [Rudolf Steiner und die Freie Hochschule für Geisteswissenschaft. English]
 Rudolf Steiner and the School for Spiritual Science : the foundation of the "first class" / Peter Selg ; [translated by Margot M. Saar].
   p. cm.
 ISBN 978-1-62148-018-1 (pbk.) — ISBN 978-1-62148-019-8 (ebook)
 1. Steiner, Rudolf, 1861–1925. 2. Freie Hochschule für Geisteswissenschaft am Goetheanum. 3. Steiner, Rudolf, 1861–1925. 4. Freie Hochschule für Geisteswissenschaft am Goetheanum—History. 5. Anthroposophy—History. 6. Wegman, Ita, 1876–1943. I. Title.
 BP595.S895S379613 2012
 299'.935—dc23

2012017963

Contents

	Preface	vii
1.	Rudolf Steiner and the School for Spiritual Science as an Esoteric Institution	1
2.	The Founding of the "First Class"	21
3.	The Contribution of Ita Wegman	43
4.	The Ritual Act and the Rose Cross	61
5.	Ita Wegman Holds the Class Lessons	79
6.	Ita Wegman's Introductory Words to the Class Lessons	101
	Appendix	113
	Notes	123

Dedicated to
Emanuel Zeylmans van Emmichoven
(1926–2008)

Preface

> *Following Rudolf Steiner's death, the mysteries cannot be revealed further at the present time, but we must continue to cultivate a living, not only rational but also ritual, continuity of the mystery contents he has given, passing them to people who did not know Rudolf Steiner and yet seek to connect with him esoterically and not just intellectually.*
> —Ludwig Count Polzer-Hoditz[1]

Since Rudolf Steiner's death in 1925, little has been written about the "First Class" of the School for Spiritual Science in Dornach. For much of the time, that was appropriate. The Class continued to live as an esoteric institution in the hearts of its disciples and in the mantras and meditations. The meditative work happened in a concealed way, in the ongoing inner striving for development of soul and spirit that appertains to any mystery school. Rudolf Steiner strictly guarded the content of the class lessons, merely intimating to the members of the General Anthroposophical Society that his Esoteric School existed and how it worked.[2] Everything else was an inherent part of the school, its rules and occult laws.

The rules Rudolf Steiner had explicitly stated were broken even in his life time; mantric contents were lost,[3] and after March 30, 1925, the First Class was drawn into dramatic conflicts that riddled the General Anthroposophical Society and remained, at least for some of the time, at the center of those conflicts.[4] Albert Steffen remarked that "in the class lessons, Rudolf Steiner gave us the most sacred gift."[5] This "most sacred gift" shared, in outer form and social impact, the fate of the twentieth century, its light and its abysmal darkness.

Johannes Kiersch looked into the conflict most recently on behalf of the Collegium of the School for Spiritual Science in Dornach. His in-depth archival research led to the publication of a comprehensive monograph (*A History of the School for Spiritual Science: The First Class,* Forest Row 2006) that relates how people handled the content of the class lessons and how, after Rudolf Steiner's death, the question as to how they should be presented gave rise to controversial claims and methods. Kiersch's foremost concern is how Steiner's words came to be read out in the class lessons, a method that does not comply, as he proposes, with Rudolf Steiner's "original intentions." Steiner clearly suggested a free use, or "free rendering," of the mantras.

Johannes Kiersch painstakingly searched public and private archives, making the outcome of his investigation available to interested readers. It is thanks to his efforts that many class members and class readers found out about the potential for conflict and tragedy attached to the class lessons in the years and decades following Rudolf Steiner's death. Members were able to read about the battles anthroposophists fought over the First Class and learned how deeply the main agents were enmeshed in the general turmoil.[6] Rudolf Steiner had stated clearly that the idea of an esoteric school, per se, relied on a particular inner quality. "Dignity, profound dignity, must prevail even in the thoughts about such a school. Only then will it be possible to bring an esoteric stream into the world today."[7] There are people who find it difficult to come to terms with Johannes Kiersch's account of the conflicts. They struggle to understand how the situation could escalate in such a dramatic way. "Dignity, profound dignity...?"

One might ask, on the other hand, whether Johannes Kiersch's book delivers what its title promises: *A History of the School for Spiritual Science: The First Class*. Kiersch writes little about the essence, the "meaning" and content of the First Class, about how Rudolf Steiner instituted the School for Spiritual Science at the Christmas Conference of 1923/24, and what he intended it to be. Kiersch hardly touches on the immense earnestness of that endeavor of an initiate in the outgoing first quarter of the twentieth century—presumably because he did not want to thematize the content of the class lessons. However, the discourse on method cannot be separated from the content and context of the esoteric lessons without considerable danger of distortion and misrepresentation. The view a person had of the delivery of the lessons might have resulted from profound study of how exactly Steiner instituted the lessons; or it might be expression of a person's particular relationship with Rudolf Steiner. Kiersch set out to write a representative history of the School for Spiritual Science and its First Class, but, since he largely ignores the class content and intentions, his book is ultimately the account of a crisis within the Anthroposophical Society.

We cannot separate the School for Spiritual Science and its First Class from Rudolf Steiner. Any historiographical endeavor must begin with his person and his spiritual work.[8] The First Class was not only Rudolf Steiner's own school; it was evidence of *his* spiritual experiences even if those experiences seemed objective and supra-personal. I would strongly question Johannes Kiersch's proposition that Rudolf Steiner "developed the School for Spiritual Science, and with it also the First Class, step by step, having observed how the individuals concerned work together."[9] The First Class was, and is, the manifestation of Rudolf Steiner's spiritual "Christian–Michaelic" path. While that path had social consequences and produced practicable forms of esoteric collaboration, it was not pursued primarily with the "individuals concerned," but in dialog with the spiritual world, its beings and powers. Obvious though this may be, it has far-reaching implications, too, with regard to the execution of the lessons. Polzer-Hoditz suggested that *one* aspect of the class lessons was to establish an "esoteric connection" with Rudolf Steiner. In reducing (as Kiersch and many others do) the reading of class lessons in their original wording to a "reliance on the past, of basing oneself on hallowed tradition with the texts that had survived"[10] and to an act of retrospection and preservation,[11] one ignores, even distorts (or conceals) an important aspect. Enunciating Rudolf Steiner's original words after intense study and penetration of the lesson content and structure was much more than, and entirely different from, taking recourse to venerable traditions.

We need to bear in mind that little is known of "Rudolf Steiner's original intentions" (Kiersch[12]) regarding the presentation of class lessons. What has been known for some time (Kiersch also documented this carefully) is that Rudolf Steiner repeatedly refused to let members see transcriptions of the class lessons; "'They simply do not exist', he would say very firmly."[13] Instead, on several occasions he encouraged work on the mantras, appointing (or confirming) responsible individuals to convey them. But did these study groups[14] or meditation groups[15] epitomize the true and single purpose of the First Class as an esoteric school with esoteric lessons that included ritual elements? Ita Wegman, who had worked closely with Rudolf Steiner and had discussed the Class with him at length, emphatically supported and encouraged such study groups after 1925, but she never saw them as being on a par with the esoteric class lessons.[16]

Preface

Rudolf Steiner held class lessons between February 15 and September 20, 1924. The lessons were taken down in shorthand by Helene Finckh with Rudolf Steiner's explicit consent. It was he who suggested to Lilly Kolisko that the lessons could be presented in their original wording to the faculty of the Waldorf school in Stuttgart.[17] Rudolf Steiner had faith in that group of people and their spiritual communion in which he partook esoterically to his last day and beyond.[18] Delving into the matter more deeply, one begins to sense why Ita Wegman and others associated the class lessons so intimately with Rudolf Steiner and why she felt that, in order to read out Rudolf Steiner's original words, one needed to be esoterically connected with him.[19] The penetration, revival and "resurrection" of Rudolf Steiner's word was for Ita Wegman not an act of "preservation" but a goal on the path of inner development; a goal that could be attained by forming an inner connection with Rudolf Steiner and that, at the same time, enhanced that connection. For Ita Wegman the holding of class lessons on the basis of Rudolf Steiner's actual words was not the same as "reading" them. It was an attempt to recreate his words out of their own esoterically awakened "I" and, therefore, an occult act that stood in the Christian–Pauline tradition and was related to the individuality of Rudolf Steiner and the First Class as a Mystery institution. "In hearing a class lesson, we experience not only an instructive lecture but also an act that can connect us with the mystery stream of all times. If we relinquish that awareness and fail to reawaken it continuously, we forfeit what Rudolf Steiner brought to Earth as a heavenly institution" (Polzer-Holditz[20]).

Johannes Kiersch, who based his research on Emanuel Zeylmans van Emmichoven's biography of Ita Wegman[21] and on other studies published in recent years by the Ita Wegman Institute, certainly went to great lengths to pay tribute to the important role Ita Wegman played in bringing about and developing the First Class.

But his claim that, in 1934/35, Ita Wegman's "inner attitude to her esoteric teaching was to change completely,"[22] that she developed "other ideas"[23] and that she—finally!—abandoned her endeavor of "protecting and preserving the original words" in favor of "free lessons" (as we know them today)[24] does not stand up to scrutiny and fails to do justice to Ita Wegman's personality. She cannot possibly be portrayed as the—late—protagonist of a practice that was hardly compatible with her intentions. There is no historical evidence that she held a single "free" class lesson. The only surviving, and very alert, witness of the class lessons Ita Wegman gave toward the end of her life (1937 to 1942)—Dr. Marianne Fiechter-Bischof (*1915)[25]—gives quite a different account. Ita Wegman was in no way opposed to working more freely with the mantra, but she was, till the end, intent on "resurrecting" Rudolf Steiner's original esoteric class lessons. The magnitude, dignity and potency of those lessons were alive for her. She would have firmly rejected the assertion that she was holding on to the past, an attitude that was—before as well as after 1935—entirely foreign to her, especially in relation to Rudolf Steiner: "*She never allowed the past to hang on her. With her all was work, all was future.... She lived only for the future*" (Liane Collot d'Herbois[26]).

Soon after March 30, 1925, Ita Wegman wrote in an essay commemorating Rudolf Steiner: "In full consciousness, but without having said a word about the future, without leaving any instructions or messages for anybody, the Master left us. When directly asked about this he firmly said 'no'."[27] Rudolf Steiner worked *right to the end* on establishing the Esoteric School. There was no one else to take on that task. Looking firmly to the future he never gave a thought to the possibility of his own death. Considering the many statements passed down from conversations with Rudolf Steiner about the holding of class lessons we must not lose sight of the fact that Rudolf Steiner said nothing about how the lessons were to be presented *after his death*. The "Esoteric School of the Goetheanum"[28] did not exist without Rudolf Steiner's person, without his spiritual research and initiation knowledge. Without all that, any use of the lesson contents was "unreal"—or left entirely to the discretion of the person in question. "Do it as you wish."[29] When Rudolf Steiner died, the School for Spiritual Science in Dornach had only just begun. He was convinced that the work done in that school was crucial for the future of humanity. He placed this work deliberately into a time threatened by a looming darkness, determined to add a second and third class to the school, despite the resistance he experienced and driven by a great sense of urgency. Although his physical health suffered a severe blow when the Goetheanum was destroyed by fire, Rudolf Steiner carried on, determined to complete what he could. He was fully involved in this work when he died. His Esoteric School remained a fragment. In Ita Wegman's view the class lessons should do justice to the obvious sacrifice Rudolf Steiner made, to his person and to the spiritual world that he served. (The class lessons were "Rudolf Steiner's final gift to us on Earth."[30]) The "spiritual substance" Rudolf Steiner provided up to March 30, 1925, needed to be internalized and transformed into a "sacrificial chalice" (out of a "longing for spiritual substance"), as Ita Wegman said. Only then could help come from the spiritual world in the future, a help that depended on the anthroposophical movement on Earth for its survival and continuity."[31] For Ita Wegman the spiritual path of absorbing the lessons—in their original wording—was a way of preparing and enabling the future, in intimate association with Rudolf Steiner's continuously active individuality. "*The passing away of the teacher can become esoteric impulse for the pupils*" (Michael Bauer[32]).

This study provides necessary additions and corrections to Johannes Kiersch's work, in regard to Ita Wegman and the "reading" of the class lessons, but also to the School for Spiritual Science and Rudolf Steiner himself. It remains a humble first sketch on a broad topic and it is to be hoped that there will be fundamental studies about the true "history" of Rudolf Steiner's School for Spiritual Science in the future. A beginning was made recently by Sergei O. Prokofieff and his impressive illustration of the path of the class lessons from the Christological point of view ("The First Class of the Michael School and its Christological Foundations," Dornach 2012). The School for Spiritual Science in Dornach was the work of an initiate. Through the esoteric collaboration of Rudolf Steiner and those who worked with him, a Christian mystery site was to be created. That aim has not been achieved yet, and intense work will be required for its realization: work carried out in awareness of the foundations laid by Rudolf Steiner, without attenuation or adaptation and in full awareness of the mystery dimension of that endeavor.

The second part of my study, which looks back to Ita Wegman as Rudolf Steiner's "helper" in the First Class, can be seen as an aspect of that wider mystery dimension.[33] It looks beyond the conflicts of the 1920s and 1930s that Ita Wegman already left behind in her lifetime: "For me the matter is settled. There are so many misunderstandings that I consider it better to leave things well alone. We all thought we were doing the right thing. Looking forward is more important now than looking back."[34]

Peter Selg
Director of the Ita Wegman Institute for
Basic Research into Anthroposophy
Arlesheim, Switzerland, July 2008

Fig. 1: The First Goetheanum

I.

Rudolf Steiner and the School for Spiritual Science as an Esoteric Institution

"In this School for Spiritual Science, all that lived in the mysteries when they flourished in the past will be re-enlivened in a form that is appropriate for our time and the future.... And once people come to think rightly about such matters in the world, they will appreciate the Goetheanum and the instrumental role it played in the renewal of the mysteries."
—Rudolf Steiner[1]

> "What we need first of all is a place that provides what cannot be found anywhere else; a place that will direct people toward the spiritual world. This, in essence, will be the content of the School for Spiritual Science."
>
> —RUDOLF STEINER[2]

On February 15, 1924, Rudolf Steiner introduced the first lesson of the *Esoteric School of the Goetheanum*[3]—or of the *First Class* of the School for Spiritual Science—with the words: "My dear friends, with this lesson I will restore to the School for Spiritual Science, as an esoteric institution, the mission that was almost torn from it in recent years."[4] He did not elaborate on this during the lesson, but said simply that "[it] will not be the task of this founding lesson to explain in detail the words just spoken. I spoke them to call attention to the significance of this lesson...."[5]

His words, spoken six weeks after the Christmas Conference of the General Anthroposophical Society, had a number of implications. When the conference was over, Rudolf Steiner instituted the School for Spiritual Science and its Sections. On February 15, 1924, in the Carpentry Building in Dornach, he said that the School for Spiritual Science had existed "esoterically" *before* the Christmas Conference and that, in the years leading up to 1924, it was almost "torn from its mission." In opening the First Class Steiner intended to reunite the school with its original purpose.

༄

Rudolf Steiner did not, in fact, speak for the first time of the School for Spiritual Science and its aims at the Christmas Conference. He had referred to it ten years earlier, when building work on the first Goetheanum (then called *Johannesbau*[6]) was just about to start. Looking back to that time, he wrote in the spring of 1924:

> The fact that, by the time building work started, Anthroposophy had attracted members who were trained and actively engaged in the most diverse scientific fields—which meant that the spiritual-scientific methods could be applied to the various sciences—made it possible for me to suggest calling it a "School for Spiritual Science."[7]

On April 6, 1914, only a few months after construction work had started, Rudolf Steiner spoke in a lecture to the Anthroposophical Society in Vienna about the current state of Anthroposophy and the intentions he pursued with the work in Dornach.

> Just as Copernican writings were on the Index even in the nineteenth century, spiritual-scientific knowledge will be eyed with suspicion by world views that are incapable of leaving behind old preconceptions and thinking patterns. It is evident now that spiritual science can inspire hearts and souls and that it is being sought. Without wanting to blow my own trumpet I can mention that there is proof that the time is ripe for spiritual science because spiritual science lies concealed in human souls: Are we not building an independent School for Spiritual Science on independent Swiss soil? And we owe it to the open-mindedness of those who support this spiritual stream that we see a monument to it being erected in an innovative architectural style, featuring a circular foundation and two cupolas, in the Dornach hills near Basel. It is the first external manifestation of what spiritual science will be able to bring to modern culture. The building is a sign that we can speak of spiritual science with much more hope and confidence despite the widespread hostilities

and incomprehension this scientific approach still faces, and has to face, in our time.[8]

༒

While the first Goetheanum was being built, Rudolf Steiner made only cautious use of the designation "School for Spiritual Science." The professional scientists among the members who would have been able to "apply the spiritual-scientific methods to the various sciences" were otherwise engaged because of the war. From the fall of 1914 onward, there could be no question of founding scientific institutes at the *Johannes Building,* but Rudolf Steiner did not abandon the idea of an academic institution. Friedrich Rittelmeyer, a Protestant priest and anthroposophist, and a highly educated and cultured man, recalled a conversation he had with Rudolf Steiner at the end of World War I: "Sometime in 1918, I said to Steiner, 'Doctor Steiner, once the war is over, we should found a research institute and try to investigate the results of spiritual-scientific research with the natural scientific means that are available. I have a few hundred Marks and know young scholars who would be up for it.' Steiner then laid both his hands on my shoulders and said with a joyfulness I rarely see in him, *'Yes, my dear doctor, let's do that!'* It was obvious in that moment what was nearest to his heart."[9]

In the years that followed, Steiner's intentions and hopes were realized only to an certain extent. The postwar social problems and the ongoing construction work at the Goetheanum devoured most of the available energy, while the economic situation continued to deteriorate. Rudolf Steiner nevertheless lectured widely on specific subjects after 1919, addressing himself to natural scientists, to the Waldorf teachers of the Stuttgart school, to physicians, theologians, educators, and artists. Considering the wide range of scientific contents and visions Steiner presented and the sheer number of potential research projects he outlined, his courses could have been a realistic starting point for a multidisciplinary academic institution. In his first course for physicians in March and April 1920, Rudolf Steiner presented a vast number of specialized themes and elaborated on their anthropological foundations, recommending suitable topics for doctoral or post-doctoral dissertations.[10]

It was not Rudolf Steiner's idea to inaugurate the Goetheanum with an academic course in the fall of 1920, nor did the idea find his unqualified approval, although he did not, in the end, object to it. ("He felt strongly...that the event should not be seen or referred to as an inauguration." Marie Savitch[11]) Rudolf Steiner's wish was to inaugurate, or "consecrate," the Goetheanum—as a mystery site—in a spiritual way with the performance of his fifth mystery drama.[12] We do not know whether he also felt that an academic course was premature in September 1920, because there was little evidence of scientific endeavor or achievement among his coworkers. Rudolf Steiner gave a series of lectures during the Goetheanum opening weeks and at the first *Hochschulkurs* (academic course) in Dornach.[13] In the two years that followed, he and other speakers in the movement contributed widely to further academic courses in Dornach, Darmstadt, Berlin, and The Hague.[14] When he spoke about the Goetheanum in Oslo on December 2, 1921, Steiner sounded hesitant:

> We have tried to found an independent School for Spiritual Science in Dornach in Switzerland. And we can say that at least *the attempt has been made* to introduce what can be gained from direct investigation of the spiritual world to the various scientific disciplines and fields of human inquiry, such as medicine, the sciences, sociology, and history—in addition to what these disciplines have already achieved with

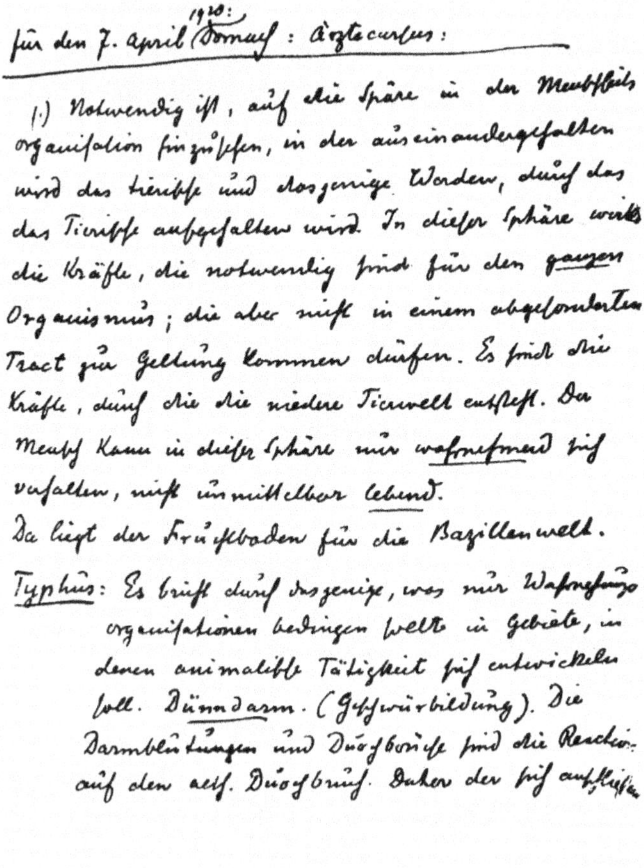

Fig. 2: Rudolf Steiner: Notes for the first medical course (1920)

their outstanding and important methods. Especially in the field of education and learning one *tries* to implement these ideas in practice in the Waldorf school in Stuttgart. Similar *attempts* have been made in the economic sphere.[15]

Rudolf Steiner struggled at least with some of the specialist lectures that were given by anthroposophists during the first academic course at the Goetheanum. Their thinking and attitude was informed by the contemporary scientific spirit, and their contributions were not suited, in either language or form, to a venue that was, as Rudolf Steiner hoped, destined to be a future mystery site.[16] Rudolf Steiner did not endeavor to achieve a synthesis of Anthroposophy and science,[17] because that was not what the world needed. He saw a need for the sciences to be imbued and transformed by spiritual science. But Steiner rarely criticized his colleagues and, for many years, kept his impressions of the first academic course in Dornach to himself.[18] He was supportive of all well-intended initiatives and left people free in their pursuits, even if, without even noticing, they failed to do justice to what Anthroposophy essentially wanted to achieve. The years after 1919 were vibrant. Many young academics discovered Anthroposophy for themselves. They came to the Goetheanum and started initiatives, devoting themselves enthusiastically to their work. But what Steiner really intended, also with his esoteric foundation, they often failed to comprehend. "People tried to model the Goetheanum on other universities."[19] The "academic affectations" and "other affectations"[20] they assumed meant that their endeavors ultimately failed to comply with the Goetheanum's designation as an *esoteric institution*. Their—often good—intentions were marred by naivety, scientific hubris, and arrogance and remained largely ineffective.

After the fire at the Goetheanum, Rudolf Steiner spoke out sharply against the fact that the much-needed spiritual-scientific work had been sacrificed to academic aspirations. Since 1919, he had, with ever-growing intensity, presented results and perspectives he had gained from his spiritual-scientific research. But his listeners took little interest, never realizing that they were called upon to take action. ("*I have certainly offered enough positive advice recently. It has not been taken up.*"[21]) Efforts to set up a "university" and offer "academic courses" continued, apparently with Rudolf Steiner's approval. In late January 1923, four weeks after the Goetheanum went up in flames, Steiner said in a crisis meeting:

> The Goetheanum is, secondly, also designated "the School for Spiritual Science," an indication that it should present scientific results. Considering the hostilities we are experiencing it is crucial that our enemies are not proved right. We cannot stand up to them with the Goetheanum—with this independent School for Spiritual Science—if they find that we produce no scientific results.... We must stand in the world truthfully, with achievements that have scientific potential. That is important, isn't it?[22]

Rudolf Steiner conceived the idea of an academic school in Dornach as early as 1913/14, envisaging it as a future mystery site from where impulses would stream into many areas of life. With the exception of his own contributions, his conception had not become reality by the time the Goetheanum perished in the blaze. The Anthroposophical Society and its headquarters in Dornach had fallen progressively under the influence of a stream that was alien to Anthroposophy.[23] "*What I really intended was increasingly dulled down by the Society, its impulsive power was sapped, especially after 1918.*"[24] After the fire, which was symptomatic, Rudolf Steiner subjected to strict scrutiny the serious shortcomings he perceived: the Society's lack of spiritual-scientific awareness, the halfhearted implementation of Anthroposophy, and the prevailing weakness for compromise and diplomacy.[25] Steiner expected anthroposophists to work courageously out of the essence and the spiritual heart of Anthroposophy—from the core of what he had for over two decades presented, lived and taught as *esotericism*. Few of the early "activists" followed him on that path after 1918, in the years when Anthroposophy made a cultural impact, although they, like the anthroposophical movement and society in their entirety, continued to admire and revere Rudolf Steiner. The year 1923 saw crisis meetings of the old society, once Rudolf Steiner had spoken out and the center of its activity in Dornach lay in ruins. But the members of the society did not change direction. Most of them failed to see where the roots of the problem lay.[26]

༄

It was in this situation that Rudolf Steiner decided, toward the end of 1923, to newly found the Anthroposophical Society and the School for Spiritual Science in Dornach. "*This might enable us to make amends for the serious wrongdoings of the past years.*"[27] He himself took on the role of chair of the Anthroposophical Society in order to represent the essence of Anthroposophy within and outside of the Society. In uniting the spiritual anthroposophical movement (as an actual spiritual being and process) with the organization and administration of the ailing Society, he performed an immensely courageous esoteric act.[28] His decision to do so was informed by the special cultural mission that fell to Anthroposophy at a time of global crises and fateful decisions: "*Looking out into the world, we realize the tremendous destructive potential that has built up for some years now. The powers we see at work give us an inkling of the abyss toward which Western civilization is headed.*"[29] A few weeks before the Christmas Conference, Adolf

Hitler attempted his first coup in Germany, following the disastrous developments that, even though they only escalated after World War I (in Germany and other European countries[30]), were ideologically rooted in the scientific materialism and agnosticism of the nineteenth century. The old Anthroposophical Society and the first Goetheanum had largely failed, but Rudolf Steiner decided, a year and a half before his death, to undertake a last resolute attempt at steering Western civilization away from the gaping abyss it was "headed toward." "*A stronger impact is needed so that the spirit that humanity needs can enter.*"[31] In numerous lectures, Steiner underlined that the spirit that was ready to enter was linked to the esoteric Christianity of the Michael age and the mystery of Christ's reappearance "in the etheric." Central European civilization had arrived at a crossroads, Steiner pointed out in 1923, and it was the mission of Anthroposophy to act on behalf of the Christ being.[32]

The Christmas Conference renewed the Anthroposophical Society and placed it in the service of the esoteric stream[33] that had always defined it.[34] Steiner pointed out on more than one occasion that the renewal of the school in Dornach as "an esoteric institution" was indeed a *foundation*. In late January 1924, four weeks after the conference in Dornach, he said in Bern:

> The School for Spiritual Science was newly *founded* at Christmas so that our Anthroposophical Society might be imbued again with esoteric life.[35]

The newly founded and renewed School for Spiritual Science in Dornach was to be the "esoteric center" of the anthroposophical movement, the "heart" and "soul" of the General Anthroposophical Society that was now one with the anthroposophical movement.

Those of Rudolf Steiner's followers who were spiritually more advanced already understood his deeper intentions in founding the school in Dornach in 1913/14. Michael Bauer, who was unable, like his friend Christian Morgenstern, to attend the laying of the foundation stone of the Johannes Building because of poor health, wrote to Morgenstern at the end of September 1913, more than ten years before the Christmas Foundation Meeting:

> *You will have heard of the laying of the foundation stone in Dornach. That we were able, at least in thought, to consciously partake in the moment when, after two thousand years of deprivation, a mystery site hallows the Earth again, must be one of the most precious moments in this life. We will, when we are born again, be sure to find our way to such a place.*[36]

The mystery dimension of the school in Dornach, which had been forced increasingly into the background after World War I, received new and special impetus from Rudolf Steiner during and after the Christmas Conference. While Rudolf Steiner never explicitly said that the Goetheanum was now a mystery site, he certainly emphasized that it could—even had to—become a mystery site if it remained true to its original orientation and mission:

> The mysteries receded when the time had come for humanity to develop freedom. Now is the time to rediscover the mysteries. Attempts need to be made now for a renewed finding of the mysteries again.
>
> The Christmas Conference took place because we know that the Earth is a place where the mysteries can be newly founded. The Anthroposophical Society must become the path that leads to the new mysteries.[37]

Elsewhere, he said in spring 1924:

> In this School for Spiritual Science, all that lived in the mysteries when they flourished in the past will be re-enlivened in a form that is appropriate for our time and the future. The

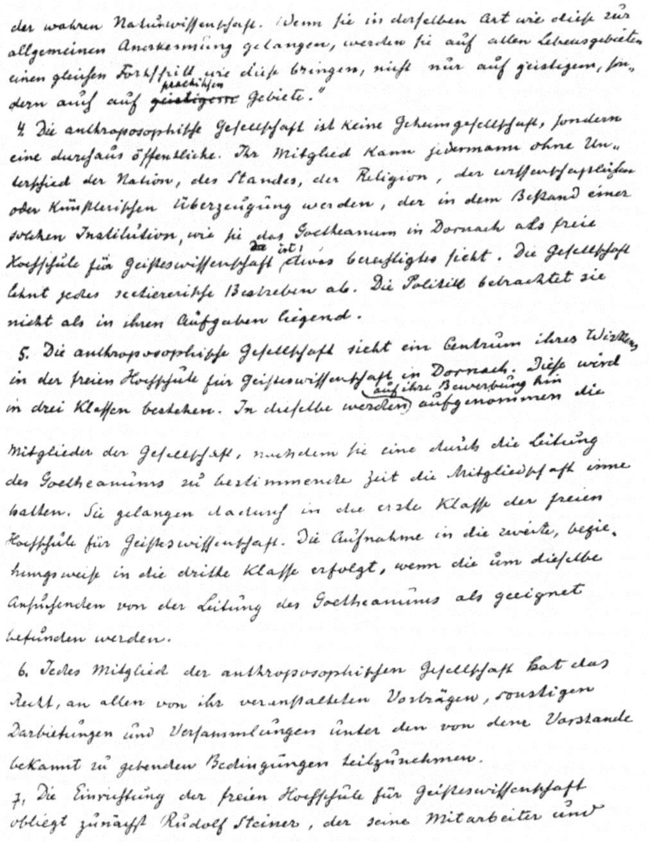

der wahren Naturwissenschaft. Wenn sie in derselben Art wie diese zur allgemeinen Anerkennung gelangen, werden sie auf allen Lebensgebieten einen gleichen Fortschritt wie diese bringen, nicht nur auf geistigem, sondern auch auf ~~geistigem~~ praktischem Gebiete."

4. Die anthroposophische Gesellschaft ist keine Geheimgesellschaft, sondern eine durchaus öffentliche. Ihr Mitglied kann jedermann ohne Unterschied der Nation, des Standes, der Religion, der wissenschaftlichen oder künstlerischen Überzeugung werden, der in dem Bestand einer solchen Institution, wie sie das Goetheanum in Dornach als freie Hochschule für Geisteswissenschaft ist, etwas Berechtigtes sieht. Die Gesellschaft lehnt jedes sektiererische Bestreben ab. Die Politik betrachtet sie nicht als in ihren Aufgaben liegend.

5. Die anthroposophische Gesellschaft sieht ein Centrum ihres Wirkens in der freien Hochschule für Geisteswissenschaft in Dornach. Diese wird in drei Klassen bestehen. In dieselbe werden auf ihre Bewerbung hin aufgenommen die Mitglieder der Gesellschaft, nachdem sie eine durch die Leitung des Goetheanums zu bestimmende Zeit die Mitgliedschaft inne hatten. Sie gelangen dadurch in die erste Klasse der freien Hochschule für Geisteswissenschaft. Die Aufnahme in die zweite, beziehungsweise in die dritte Klasse erfolgt, wenn die um dieselbe Ansuchenden von der Leitung des Goetheanums als geeignet befunden werden.

6. Jedes Mitglied der anthroposophischen Gesellschaft hat das Recht, an allen von ihr veranstalteten Vorträgen, sonstigen Darbietungen und Versammlungen unter den vom Vorstande bekannt zu gebenden Bedingungen teilzunehmen.

7. Die Einrichtung der freien Hochschule für Geisteswissenschaft obliegt zunächst Rudolf Steiner, der seine Mitarbeiter und

Fig. 3: Rudolf Steiner: The statutes of the Anthroposophical Society mysteries had passed their climax when the greatest mystery in the history of the world took place in a most concealed manner: the Mystery of Golgotha. The time came when, and because, the mysteries had withdrawn from the spiritual evolution of humanity; humankind had to become increasingly absorbed in the evolutionary stream that would give them freedom. Now it is time for the mysteries to come back to life, in the truest sense of the word and in a form that is appropriate for our times. And once people come to think rightly about such matters in the world, they will appreciate the Goetheanum and the instrumental role it played in the renewal of the mysteries.[38]

Rudolf Steiner explained at the Christmas Conference that renewing the mysteries implied finding access to the spiritual world. The Esoteric School, he said, needed to work methodically with the spiritual path from which it had grown. He concluded the final lecture of that momentous meeting with these words:

> Here in Dornach must be the place where one can speak to people who want to hear about all important and immediate experiences one can have in the spiritual world. Here, we must find the strength to not just vaguely indicate in the theoretical, dialectic–empirical way so typical of today's science that traces of a spiritual world might be found here or there. If Dornach wants to be true to its mission we have to speak openly about what happens in the spiritual world, about the spiritual impulses entering our lives and prevailing in nature. Here, it must be possible to speak of real spiritual experiences, powers and beings. Dornach must be the school of true spiritual science. And we must no longer be in awe of today's sciences that will lead humanity before the earnest Guardian of the Threshold in a state of sleep. We have to find the strength here in Dornach to come eye-to-eye—spiritually speaking—with the spiritual world and to learn about the spiritual world.[39]

A few weeks later, Rudolf Steiner described the significance and mission of the future school in a brief summary:

> What we need, first of all, is a place that provides what cannot be found anywhere else; a place that will direct people toward the spiritual world. That, in essence, will be the content of the School for Spiritual Science.[40]

At the Christmas Conference and in the months that followed, Rudolf Steiner placed the Esoteric School of the Goetheanum, which consisted of three classes, at the center of the foundation in Dornach. The School for Spiritual Science, as he pointed out, was identical with this Esoteric School. As a place of spiritual research and teaching, as an esoteric institution, it was the heart of the Goetheanum. Nine months after the conference Rudolf Steiner said:

> This truly anthroposophic Esoteric School must *take the place* of the independent School for Spiritual Science that was first envisaged but failed. The new school must represent the core of the Anthroposophical Society's esoteric activity.[41]

This statement might be confusing owing to Rudolf Steiner's use of the name "School for Spiritual Science." The academic institution he initiated in the spring of 1914 began as a multidisciplinary school of higher education and research in which "*spiritual-scientific methods were applied to the various sciences*" (Steiner). How, then, could he refer, during and after the Christmas Conference, to the newly founded three-class Esoteric School of the Goetheanum as an institution that would "*take the place*" of the former "independent School for Spiritual Science," while holding on to the academic concept? ("The independent School for Spiritual Science at the Goetheanum... will be an esoteric school."[42]) For many members of Rudolf Steiner's audience that remained an open question for a long time. Steiner merely indicated that he saw the "Sections" (faculties) of the School for Spiritual Science in Dornach as part of the actual Esoteric School. The "esoteric movement" was "organized in sections"[43] that would differentiate the esoteric essence, he said,[44] and the Esoteric School was *"divided into sections."*[45]

Steiner's almost cryptic remarks have as yet hardly been penetrated. His meaning can be elucidated if we look at the Medical Section of the School for Spiritual Science and how it evolved during Rudolf Steiner's chairmanship. He called medicine "the most important practical application of human knowledge."[46] Owing to the particular situation at the time, Rudolf Steiner was able to follow up the Christmas Conference with two methodical training courses for physicians and medical students.[47] The courses were mantric in structure and included esoteric content.[48] Before the beginning of the second course, Rudolf Steiner admitted all members of the course as a group to the First Class or Esoteric School of the Goetheanum.[49] There are passages in the lectures Steiner gave during that course that, in spirit and structure, closely resemble esoteric lessons. With Ita Wegman, the leader of the Medical Section, Rudolf Steiner sent out a newsletter to the course members, and he referred to that letter in a class lesson, explaining that he would send out such newsletters[50] to inform the members of the School for Spiritual Science about the *"ongoing work of the school."* All class members should be aware of what *"streams through this school in Dornach."*[51] The content of this particular newsletter was of a medical nature and the "ongoing work of the school" was, in this case, Rudolf Steiner's (and Ita Wegman's) medical research. Rudolf Steiner saw clearly the spiritual work carried out in the various faculties or sections as part of the Esoteric School. Rudolf Steiner's specialist research and his

Goetheanum, den 11. März 1924

Liebe Freunde!

Unseren, einem Versprechen gleichkommenden Mitteilungen über die Führung der medizinischen Sektion am Goetheanum, die wir gelegentlich der Weihnachtstagung gemacht haben, nachkommend, senden wir an die für die Pflege des Medizinischen mit uns Verbundenen diesen ersten Rundbrief. Er ist getragen von der Gesinnung, die uns bei den medizinischen Kursen im Neujahr vereingte. Er möchte am liebsten jedem Worte etwas mitgeben, von den Gefühlen für die leidende Menschheit, aus dem allein nicht nur die Hingabe an die Heilkunst, sondern auch deren wirkliche Kraft hervorgehen muss.

    Es war in alten Zeiten
    Da lebte in der Eingeweihten Seelen
    Kraftvoll der Gedanke, dass krank
    Von Natur ein jeglicher Mensch sei.
    Und Erziehen ward angesehen
    Gleich dem Heilprozess
    Der dem Kinde mit dem Reifen
    Die Gesundheit zugleich brachte
    Für des Lebens vollendetes Menschsein.

Es ist gut, solch kraftvolle Gedanken, gewonnen aus der Anschauung alter instinktiver Weisheit, sich vor die Seele treten zu lassen, wenn man in rechter innerlicher Sammlung die Seele bereiten will zum Erfassen der Heileswirkungen.

Vergessen wir nicht, dass dem Heilprozesse eine Seele mitgegeben werden muss, daß er nicht nur an einen Körper, sondern auch an eine Seele sich wenden muss. Je mehr solche Gedanken die junge Aerzte begreifen, desto mehr wird in das medizinische Leben das einfliessen, was der sinnige Arzt sehnsüchtig verlangt, wenn er den heutigen Stand seiner Kunst mit den Grenzen empfindet, was der Kranke wie eine Gnade empfinden wird, wenn er es im Heilprozess erlebt.

Liebe Freunde, Ihr habt, so weit Ihr im Januar hier versammelt wart, offenen Herzens entgegen genommen, was aus solcher Gesinnung an Euch herantreten wollte. Uns wird unvergesslich sein, wie aus Euern Augen dies gesprochen, aus Euern warmen Worten zu uns gedrungen ist. Unsere Gedanken weilen bei Euch, und sie sollen heute zum ersten Male in Anknüpfung an Eure gestellten Fragen zu Euch hinwandeln.

Wir senden das Folgende an einzelne Adressen und bitten diejenigen, die von uns direkte Sendung erhalten, dafür zu sorgen, dass sie weiter gehen an die von uns mitgeteilten Adressen.

*Fig. 4: Rudolf Steiner/Ita Wegman:
draft for the* Medical Newsletter. *April 1924*

collaboration as an initiate with the section leaders formed the center of each section's spiritual research and teaching. From this center (which was not public), spiritual-scientific support would flow to the various specialist fields: initiation knowledge, research methods and assignments, as well as forms of inner development that would benefit members of the School for Spiritual Science in their own field of expertise, and through them the world at large. "We want to remain united, my dear friends, so that you will continue to have your center here in Dornach at the Goetheanum and that *this center can, through you, work into the world.*"[52] The Goetheanum was to have an effect on the civilization of the world. As with the ancient mystery sites, impulses were to stream from the Goetheanum into the various areas of civilization—from the center of initiation into the world—facilitated by associative esoteric communities.

Illness prevented Rudolf Steiner from establishing the second and third class of his Esoteric School and from building up the sections of the School for Spiritual Science as envisaged. With the exception of the General Anthroposophical Section, where the nineteen class lessons had been given, esoteric section work had, strictly speaking, not begun yet in the fall of 1924[53] if we discount the initial paradigmatic attempts in medicine, research,[54] publishing,[55] and teaching.[56] Rudolf Steiner's lectures to the young physicians and medical students were practically the beginning of the "Medical Mystery School," for which Ita Wegman had asked Rudolf Steiner in the summer of 1924.[57] This mystery school for medicine was in harmony with the orientation of the Medical Section and the School for Spiritual Science. ("Attempts must be made now to find the mysteries again.") With the help of Ita Wegman, Rudolf Steiner was still able, in the second half of September 1924, to establish the Medical Mystery School with the members of the "course for young doctors." By performing a special ritual act that included a solemn pledge spoken in his studio, in front of the Christ Statue, Rudolf Steiner founded the "esoteric core of the Medical Section."[58]

Owing to his illness, Rudolf Steiner could not give the lessons intended to transform the first esoteric section in Dornach into a medical mystery school. But his whole demeanor revealed how he envisaged the future School for Spiritual Science. *"That the School for Spiritual Science with its various sections must become the esoteric core for everything that is to work esoterically in the Anthroposophical Society"*[59] transpired in the nine months of intense work following the Christmas Conference up until the time when Rudolf Steiner fell ill, because he kept the members informed about this work through his written reports. The foundation for his efforts and mainstay of the entire multidisciplinary School for Spiritual Science was, however, the First Class of the General Anthroposophical Section and its esoteric lessons. (*"It is there for all who seek to deepen their soul life."*[60])

Fig. 5: Rudolf Steiner

2.

The Founding of the "First Class"

"Receive this school as an institution willed by the spiritual world. We need to interpret this will in a way that is suitable for our age. Our age began when the darkness ended and a light reappeared. This light is still barely visible on Earth, because humanity is holding on to the old darkness. But the light is there. And only if we comprehend that the light is there will we grasp the true essence and intention of our spiritual school."

—RUDOLF STEINER [1]

Rudolf Steiner did not follow his own impulse when, early in 1924, he instituted the Esoteric School of the Goetheanum with its three classes: *"Esoteric schools...are not rooted in the earthly realm. They exist only as earthly reflections of institutions founded in suprasensory worlds."*² A true esoteric school, Rudolf Steiner said, was the "earthly image of a spiritual institution;"³ it served the spiritual world and the spiritual world nurtured and maintained it:

> The spiritual world [needs to] manifest its willingness to create such a school. We cannot decide arbitrarily to create an esoteric school, not even if our human arbitrariness is of the kind referred to as "human ideals." An esoteric school must be a body that receives impulses from spiritual life. What happens in an esoteric school is expression of suprasensory events in the spiritual world.⁴

The Esoteric School of the Goetheanum was "willed in full earnestness" by the spiritual world;⁵ "willed by the spiritual powers that rule over the world today."⁶ It was created early in 1924 as an "institution of the spiritual world for our time"⁷ under the influence of the "light" that had returned in the "Age of Light."

Rudolf Steiner's Anthroposophy was a kind of a "mystery being" and therefore subject, in appearance and effect, to mystery laws. ("The anthroposophical movement is not here because it pleases us. It is here because the spiritual powers that govern the world and direct human history deem the time right for the spirit light, which can be conveyed through Anthroposophy, to permeate human civilization in a way that is appropriate to the times."⁸) These conditions applied in a particular way to the anthroposophically inspired "Esoteric School of the Goetheanum." The school was a spiritual "institution." Rudolf Steiner could not act and decide in it as he wished. The "institution" of the school had to be directed from the "spiritual world itself"[9] and was preceded by the "plea," or "request," presented by Rudolf Steiner:

> The counsel of the spiritual world has been obtained in the appropriate way.[10]

> The school is a spiritual institution; it was founded after listening to what the spiritual powers that govern the world deemed right for humanity in our time.[11]

In early February 1917, seven years before the Esoteric School of the Goetheanum was established, Rudolf Steiner explained in a lecture to members in Berlin that Anthroposophy was in a singular way suited to speaking out and asking profound questions. Anthroposophy made it possible for us to consult the Christ being, especially before important decisions and foundations:

> Because of Christ's appearance and presence the time will come when people will learn to approach him, not only when they have questions concerning their own soul life, but also when they want to found something here on Earth, with the immortal part of their individuality. Christ is not only the ruler over humanity; he is also our brother and he wants us to consult him on all questions of life, especially in times like those that lie ahead of us.... Life being what it is today, people seem as far removed from the Christ as they can possibly be. Who of us ever asks in a time like ours: What does Christ Jesus say to this? Some say they do, but it would be blasphemous to believe that they truly ask it, that the questions they ask are truly addressed to the Christ. The time must come now for immortal human souls, who want to found something, to ask the Christ when the time is right for this foundation—when human souls recognize the Christ as a loving companion in their life who bestows on them not

only comfort and strength, but advice on how to proceed. The kingdom of Christ Jesus is not of this world, but it must be active in this world, and human souls must be the instruments of the kingdom that is not of this world. We must be aware of how little the Christ is consulted today on questions concerning people's individual endeavors and undertakings. But we must learn to consult the Christ. How can we do it? We must learn to speak his language. Anyone who comprehends the true purpose of spiritual science, will recognize that it is more than a body of theoretical knowledge about problems of humanity, the layers of human nature, reincarnation, and karma. They will try to discover the particular language it has to give expression to spiritual matters. Learning to converse inwardly with the spiritual world through spiritual science is much more important for us than acquiring theoretical knowledge. For the Christ is with us always, even to the end of earthly time. We must learn to speak his language.... Through spiritual science, we teach ourselves a language that can express the questions we want to ask the spiritual world. And if we work inwardly on this language of spiritual life, we will find that the Christ is with us, answering our questions. This is what we should gain from our spiritual-scientific endeavors as inner disposition, as a sentiment or feeling. Why do we study spiritual science? We do it to learn the vocabulary that we need to draw closer to Christ. By learning to penetrate the world and its secrets with spiritual science, we invite the Christ Jesus to rise from the dim, dark foundations of world mysteries and bestow on us the strength we need in life. The Christ will be with us as our brother, and he will guide us so that we can be strong in heart and soul to tackle the future tasks of human evolution.

We must, therefore, not absorb spiritual science as a doctrine, but as a language and wait until, in this language, we can find the questions we want to ask the Christ. He will answer! There is no doubt that he will answer! We therefore need to acquire spiritual science, not only as a doctrine but also as language, and we need to learn to find in that language the questions we can address to the Christ. He will answer; yes, he will answer! And if, out of the grey spiritual depths through which humanity passes right now, we hear the counsel that Christ will bestow very soon on those who seek it, we will receive the soul forces, the soul strength and the soul impulses we need.[12]

Seven years later, in mid-February 1924, Rudolf Steiner held the first Class Lesson of the School for Spiritual Science in Dornach. He had the support of the spiritual beings "who are close to the Earth and strive to save humanity."[13] They are the spiritual beings that agreed to the founding of the school. On the following day, February 16, 1924, Rudolf Steiner began in Dornach with the great cycle of karma lectures that arose from and increasingly thematized the Michael Mystery. From the summer of 1924, Rudolf Steiner referred explicitly to Michael—the "Countenance of Christ," the reigning spirit of time who acts on behalf of the Christ being—as the leader of the Esoteric School of the Goetheanum. On August 2, he said, *"We now stand before the anthroposophical school that was founded by Michael."*[14] Steiner took almost six months to prepare the members of his school and those who heard the karma lectures before he could pronounce openly and directly:

> We could not create this Esoteric School without consulting the power that, as I have often pointed out here in lectures to members, has directed the spiritual life of humanity as Michael since the last third of the nineteenth century.[15]

"Michael's power itself" had instituted the Esoteric School of the Goetheanum. As Rudolf Steiner explained in the summer and fall of 1924,[16] Michael was the school's "true leader."[17] He inspired and directed his school as the "Michael School of the present,"[18]

The Founding of the "First Class"

*Fig. 6: Rudolf Steiner: "The Figure of Christ"
(wood sculpture, 1917–1925)*

in accordance with the "signs of the time" and the "light" that had reappeared. Rudolf Steiner demanded of the school's members that they not only embraced that truth in an intellectual way but also made it wholly their own:

> And, my dear friends, you will only comprehend what is said in this school if you know that everything that is said here is meant to be brought to humanity in our time by the Michael stream. The words spoken in this school are Michael words. The will expressed in this school is Michael will. All of you, who are rightful members of this school, are disciples of Michael. You must know this deep inside to be a true pupil of this school, to sit here with the right inner attitude and to feel that you are a member not of an earthly institution but of a heavenly institution that enters the world.[19]

The "contents" of the esoteric class lessons would "make sense" only if the school was imbued with the "Michael stream" and if it remained connected with that stream.[20] Rudolf Steiner spoke in more depth about the "Michael stream" in his karma lectures[21] and wrote extensively about it in essays, even during his final illness.[22]

❦

Endowed with the power of the Michael age, Rudolf Steiner acted as the earthly leader of the Esoteric School of the Goetheanum.[23] As initiates had always done in their respective mystery schools, he spoke as the "representative of the spiritual powers of the world."[24] He made the school visible on Earth; through him it became a real social institution that conveyed true "communications from the spiritual world."[25] *"If you become a member of this school you meet the spiritual world face to face."*[26]

Rudolf Steiner had spiritual responsibility for the school toward the Christ–Michael power that had facilitated its institution. Through his person the mantra resounded in the esoteric lessons. "On behalf of Michael," Rudolf Steiner imparted the mantric words of the "Guardian of the Threshold to the spiritual world" to the members of the school.[27] Rudolf Steiner referred to the "Guardian of the Threshold" as a "servant of the Michael power,"[28] as the "earnest and first representative of Michael."[29] Members who chose to embark on the path of esoteric development had to confront this true "servant of Michael at the threshold to the spirit land."[30] Rudolf Steiner spoke the mantras, but introduced them by saying:

> It is not I who speaks them; I speak them on behalf of the Guardian of the Threshold, who wants to speak these words to you through me.[31]

Rudolf Steiner said that the "Guardian of the Threshold" acted "at the behest of Michael"; that the power of Michael was streaming into the Esoteric School, "blessing" and "enhancing" its rites and contents. "With his power, spirit and love"[32] Michael was present in the lessons whose founder and holder he was.[33] As a genuine "Michael proclamation" in the "Age of Light" (which began in 1899), the school was under his "immediate influence."

> Receive this school as an institution willed by the spiritual world. We need to interpret this will in a way that is suitable for our age. Our age began when the darkness ended and a light reappeared. This light is still barely visible on Earth because humanity is holding on to the old darkness. But the light is there. And only if we comprehend that the light is there, will we grasp the true essence and intention of our spiritual school.[34]

Rudolf Steiner designated the "Spiritual School of the Goetheanum" also a "*Michaelic Rosicrucian School*,"[35] a school that combined the power of Michael with the spiritual endeavor of

Rosicrucianism, the esoteric Christian movement led by Christian Rosenkreutz.[36]

Through the school (and led by their own destiny), the members of the "Michaelic Rosicrucian School" found access to a higher, suprasensory community that was and is "guided and led" by Michael himself.[37] In the early summer of 1924 Rudolf Steiner began to speak explicitly of this Michael community in his karma lectures. At the end of the nineteenth—and final—First Class Lesson he said with a view to the past and the future:

> My dear sisters and brothers, as you heard in the general anthroposophical lectures, it was in Michael's suprasensory school that these intimate teachings of the heart first reverberated. Powerful images of the imaginative cult of the early nineteenth century were then placed before those chosen to be close to Michael, as revelations from the fifteenth, sixteenth, and seventeenth centuries of the school that was led in the suprasensory world by Michael and his host. We now stand before this anthroposophical school, founded by Michael. We feel we belong to it. Michael words are required to describe the path that leads into the spiritual world and into the human "I." These Michael words of the esoteric Michael School constitute the first division.
>
> When we, as needs to be confirmed, come together again for these class lessons in September, the imaginative ritual revelations of the early nineteenth century will first be described, according to the will of the Michael power. That will constitute the second division. The mantric words that have entered our souls will continue to stand as images before our inner eye. These images will—to the extent possible—be images conjured down from the suprasensory imaginative cult of the early nineteenth century.
>
> The third chapter of this school will lead us directly to the interpretations given for the mantric words in the

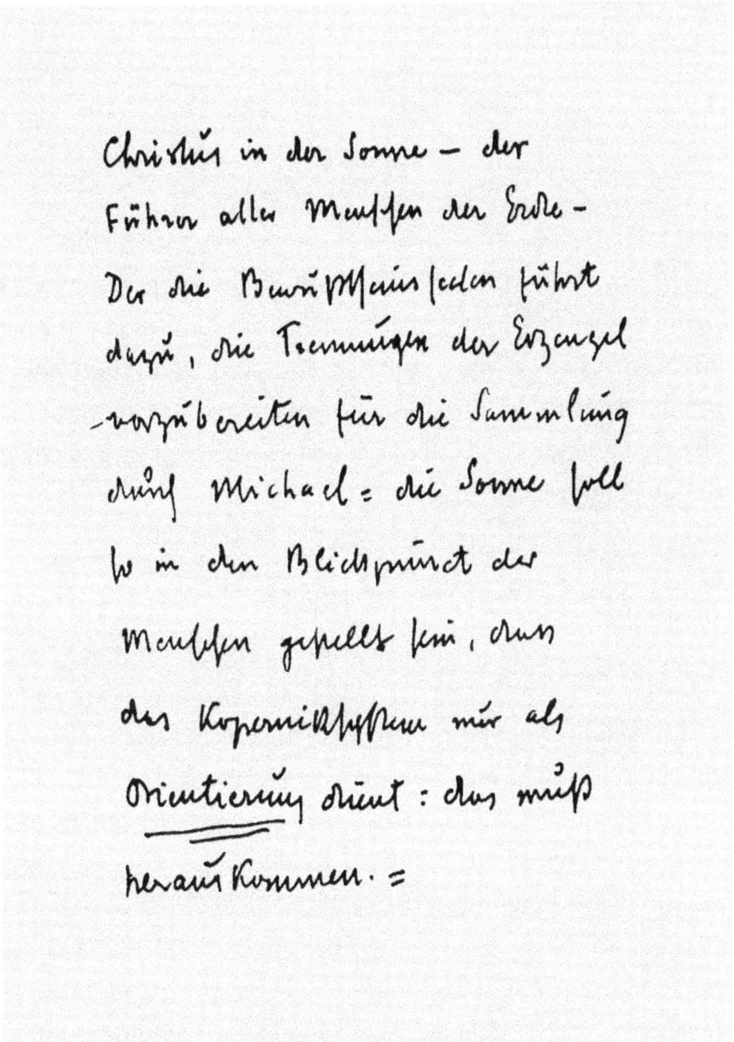

Christus in der Sonne – der
Führer aller Menschen der Erde –
Der die Bewusstseinsseelen führt
dazu, die Trennungen der Erzengel
vorzubereiten für die Sammlung
durch Michael = die Sonne soll
so in den Blickpunkt der
Menschen gestellt sein, dass
das Kopernikussystem nur als
Orientierung dient: das muss
herauskommen. =

Fig. 7: Rudolf Steiner: Notes for a karma lecture, Arnhem, July 18-20, 1924 suprasensory Michael School of the fifteenth, sixteenth and seventeenth centuries.[38]

Rudolf Steiner did not live to open the second and third "chapters" of the school.

☙

In the First Class of the Esoteric School of the Goetheanum, Rudolf Steiner introduced in nineteen lessons the *"practice of cognition."*[39] The class lessons should convey an "image" of what one experiences on penetrating the spiritual world. They should include elements of imagination, inspiration and intuition to allow members to relive the spiritual experiences in their own thinking and feeling:

> The school will guide its members up to spiritual realms that cannot be conveyed through ideas. One needs to find the means of expressing imaginations, inspirations and intuitions.[40]

The class lessons of the esoteric "school for spiritual development"[41] were the earnest attempt to embark on the etheric-Rosicrucian path of spiritual development that Rudolf Steiner had taught systematically for two decades, a path that only few had walked successfully. *"The esoteric deepening that you find described in detail in my book* How to Know Higher Worlds, *and that is much discussed, will now be facilitated in the three classes."*[42] "Every human heart that is honest with itself"[43] longed for that kind of spiritual deepening that was not easily achieved. Success depended entirely on whether or not one was able to *"understand what it means to live in an existence that is not conveyed through our senses or physical organization; to live, as it were, in the sphere of soul and spirit that constitutes our true being."*[44]

Since the beginning of the twentieth century Rudolf Steiner had frequently remarked on the veritable "abyss" that separates the world of the physical senses from that of pure spirit (as well as on the different ways in which these worlds are experienced). According to Rudolf Steiner our soul needs to undergo profound transformative processes before it can enter the spiritual world. To achieve this transformation we have to confront the figure known from ancient tradition—and described by Steiner early on—as the "Guardian of the Threshold."[45] The lessons of the First Class are largely the content of *"what can be learned in conversation with the Guardian of the Threshold"*[46]—that is, they form part of an initiate's spiritual autobiography. Those who do not have immediate access to the spiritual world, but seek to gain it, can have an initial experience of the path of initiation into the spiritual world by means of the esoteric lessons and the images and verses presented there. They can strive to gain a true "image" of what the soul needs to go through before it can make the transition to the purely spiritual, suprasensory world in a healthy and unalienated way. We only need to internalize and actively work with the images and mantras from the Class to transform our soul forces. We will realize how distorted these soul forces are in our times and learn how they can be employed to gain knowledge of the spiritual world.[47] The esoteric lessons of the First Class are without doubt a kind of mystery preschool because they make us aware of the deficiency of our present existence and awaken us to the essential qualities our spirit-soul unfolds when it can associate with higher powers.

This association with the higher powers that can be achieved in the Esoteric School was and is a way of "finding the world through self-knowledge" and therefore a path toward the experience of cosmic reality.[48] According to Rudolf Steiner all ancient mystery teaching involved the enhanced experience of the elementary world as a bridge from microcosmic to macrocosmic existence. The Esoteric School of the Goetheanum taught this path through Rudolf Steiner. With his instructions to "young physicians and medical students" Steiner demonstrated in the Medical Section of the School for Spiritual Science how essential spiritual experiences were for a diagnostic and therapeutic practice based on spiritual science.[49] In the First Class lessons, Rudolf Steiner led his listeners ever more deeply into the sphere of the spiritual hierarchies, the spirit realm where souls dwell after crossing the "threshold": *Here on Earth we communicate with the beings of the three nature kingdoms and with other people. Over there we communicate with the disembodied souls and the spirits of the higher hierarchies.*"[50] Through meditation on the esoteric lessons we can, according to Rudolf Steiner, gain access to the inner world of the hierarchies and witness the "heavenly conversations" of higher entities. We can enter the "kingdom of truth"[51] and of "true reality"[52] where we will experience our true self in the realm of the first hierarchy:

> What we see as our I in the natural world is but a vain outer reflection of our true I that lives among the higher hierarchies. As soon as we gain true self-knowledge we must enter the sphere of the higher hierarchies where we cannot but witness their communications.[53]

The inner path of the class lessons consequently prepares us also for life after earthly death. It is a meeting with our own "I" and our karmic potential in the presence of the higher hierarchies. The spiritual experiences presented in the class lessons describe the earthly path of inner spiritual development. This development consists in a voluntary temporary detachment from our physical organization necessary for gaining suprasensory knowledge. The experiences also reflect the life of the excarnated soul after death.

"When we pass through the gate of death and enter transcendental life to live in the reality of the spiritual worlds; when we dwell in the world of the angeloi, archangeloi, exusiai, dynamis, kyriotetes, seraphim, cherubim, thrones; when we experience all that, it is important that we remember what we learned through initiation science when we still lived on Earth, for without that our after-death experiences will remain unfathomable and dark to us."[54] After reading out the mantra in the eighteenth—and penultimate—Class Lesson, Rudolf Steiner said:

> Those people who heard this in esoteric lessons will pass through the gate of death and hear how the same words resound over there. They will hear how the Esoteric School here and life between death and a new birth over there resound together. And they will understand what they hear.
>
> But there are people who are resistant and unwilling to open themselves to the contents conveyed by the esoteric schools after the general introduction to Anthroposophy. They will not hear what initiation science bestows on them from the higher realms. They will pass through the gate of death and hear what they should have heard on Earth. And they will not comprehend it. The powerful words shared by the gods will be mere sound to them, mere cosmic noise.
>
> We can read about it in the Gospels, and Paul speaks of it when he says that we can protect ourselves from death in the land of spirits if we listen to the teachings of the Christ. It is paramount to death in the spirit land if we pass through the gate of death and fail to understand what we hear there; if we do not hear the meaningful words of gods but only incomprehensible noise because our soul died instead of gaining eternal life. We have initiation science so that souls continue to live. We have esoteric schools so that our souls will live on when we pass through the gate of death. We must take in what these schools teach us.[55]

Rudolf Steiner's intention in founding the Esoteric School of the Goetheanum was to create a spiritual center for the School for Spiritual Science but also to raise a *"rock of strength for Anthroposophy."*[56] In doing so he hoped to regenerate the General Anthroposophical Society as the tool that would enable Anthroposophy to work on the whole of civilization from out of the new Esoteric School. Although Anthroposophy had attracted growing interest since 1918, it had also undergone a process of alienation caused by the partial failing of the Anthroposophical Society (or rather, of its administrative organs). In 1924, Rudolf Steiner said to the members of the "First Class":

> Carelessness, in particular, has taken its toll on the Anthroposophical Society in recent years. Overcoming that tendency will be the task, or one of the tasks, of the members of this school.[57]

Rudolf Steiner spoke repeatedly of the "absolute earnestness" and "active earnestness" needed in the Esoteric School and in the anthroposophical movement as a whole. He suffered immensely from the fact that the Christmas Conference, its inner dimension and meaning for the future, had only been partly understood and taken hold of.[58] He expected members of the School for Spiritual Science to live through the Christmas Conference in full consciousness and even made membership in the school dependent on the applicants' commitment in that respect. On February 3, 1924, just two weeks before the first Class Lesson, he said: *"The members of the First Class must form a society of anthroposophical earnestness. Much of what the Christmas Conference introduced has not risen to people's consciousness yet."*[59] Half a year later he said:

The esoteric members of the Esoteric School constitute a core group of human beings who must be educated to gradually acquire the necessary earnestness.[60]

The entire Goetheanum was in fact dedicated to humanity and consciously placed by Rudolf Steiner in the twentieth century. In the third decade of a century that would witness an unleashing of evil powers without precedence in the history of humanity he founded the "Michael School of our time" as the Goetheanum's esoteric center. Rudolf Steiner was able to read the signs of the time as a result of his spiritual-scientific research. The Esoteric School of the Goetheanum was to prepare its members for what lay ahead.[61] Rudolf Steiner not only warned the members of the School for Spiritual Science that "[we] must learn to comprehend the full earnestness of esotericism."[62] He predicted that a "difficult journey" lay before them and before civilization in general. In the second esoteric lesson, given on February 22, 1924 (Ita Wegman's 48th birthday), Rudolf Steiner underlined the word "evil" three times in a mantra. Elsewhere he said:

> Difficult times lie ahead for Anthroposophy and the members of the school must know that they will have to cope with these challenges. You are not just anthroposophists; you are members of an esoteric school.[63]

According to Rudolf Steiner it did not suffice for members of the Esoteric School to "listen" to Anthroposophy. They were asked to represent Anthroposophy exoterically, "before the world," also in difficult times: *"I am a representative of Anthroposophy which emanates from the Goetheanum."*[64] There is no doubt that Rudolf Steiner foresaw the evils of Fascism and the Second World War, possibly also the resistance and sacrifices that the anthroposophical community would face. At Easter 1924, half a year after the Nazis' attempt at

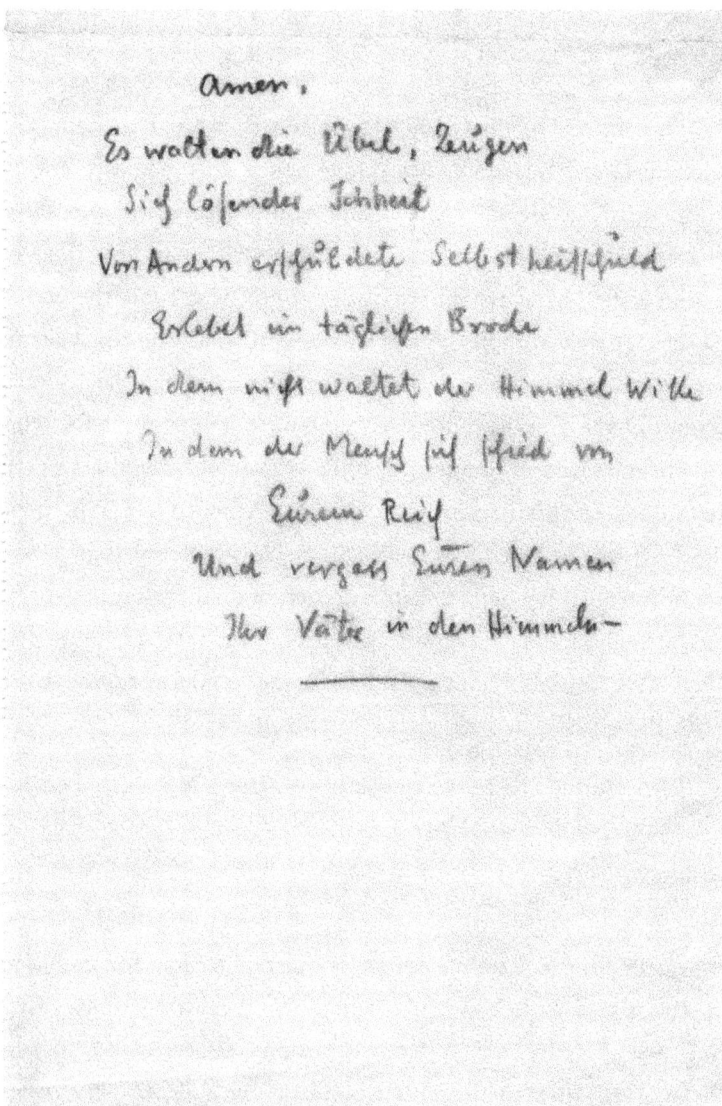

Fig. 8: "The reverse Lord's Prayer" in Rudolf Steiner's handwriting

overthrowing the government, Rudolf Steiner read a text about the developments in Germany in a class lesson and spoke of the dangers awaiting the Anthroposophical Society and the Christian Community, eleven and seventeen years respectively before they were banned by Adolf Hitler:

> With a movement that is rooted in the spirit it is indeed not a matter of how many members it has, my dear friends, but it is a matter of what kind of power inhabits it from out of the spiritual world. The adversaries see that great power and therefore they choose not light but heavy armor.[65]

Aware of this historical constellation and of the tasks awaiting the members of his Esoteric School, Rudolf Steiner wanted them to really understand the "serious spirit" and the "holy earnestness" involved in founding the School for Spiritual Science. He excluded several members after they violated the school's regulations. He warned repeatedly that the esoteric knowledge could lose its power if members did not cultivate the appropriate inner attitude ("*Such a school with the necessary esoteric earnestness can only survive if its members meet the requirements posed by the spiritual powers that preside over it.*"[66]) In the same context he spoke about choosing one's words wisely:

> We must feel responsible even for the words we choose. We must feel responsible for each word we utter and examine it most earnestly to see whether we can vouch for its truth. Untrue statements, however well-intended they may be, work destructively on occult movements. We must not deceive ourselves on that point; we must be very clear about it. It is not the intentions that count—people tend to not take them seriously enough—but the objective truth. It is one of the foremost duties of esoteric students that they not only commit to what they believe to be true but examine if what they say is objectively true. Only if we serve the

divine-spiritual powers that inspire this school and understand what is objectively true will we be able to safely navigate the difficulties that await Anthroposophy.⁶⁷

Fig. 9: Ita Wegman, March 21, 1925

3.

The Contribution of Ita Wegman

"*On September 5, 1924, I was admitted to the First Class by Rudolf Steiner. After the handshake that was a pledge of loyalty, at the same time he asked me to take the hand of Dr. Wegman, his coleader, who was sitting next to him.*"[1]

> "She [Ita Wegman] did not just want to carry on traditions. She asked the crucial Parcival question as to a new esotericism. The question in itself and how it was asked enabled me to establish the Michael School on Earth. This school holds the seed of the future."
>
> —RUDOLF STEINER[2]

Rudolf Steiner told Ludwig Count Polzer-Hoditz that the physician Ita Wegman had asked him for the "new esotericism"—or a new esoteric school. The request was probably made in Penmaenmawr in Wales, where Steiner gave a lecture course on initiation wisdom in the summer of 1923.[3] *"The question in itself and how it was asked enabled me to establish the Michael School on Earth."* Before the First Class could be instituted, the decisive question needed to be asked by someone who had a close connection with Rudolf Steiner and his work. Once the request was made Rudolf Steiner could actively approach the spiritual world. "The counsel of the spiritual world was obtained with the appropriate means."[4] "The school is a spiritual institution; it was established after the spiritual powers that rule the world had been consulted on what was appropriate for humanity in our time."[5]

Ita Wegman was an early esoteric pupil of Rudolf Steiner's. From the fall of 1905 she was a member of the "Esoteric School" that was part of the German Section of the Theosophical Society. Rudolf Steiner had begun to establish the Esoteric School, which also consisted of three classes, in Germany in the summer of 1904.[6] Like all its members, Ita Wegman attended Rudolf Steiner's esoteric lessons, received personal exercises and mantras from him for her meditative work,[7] and spoke with her teacher about her inner experiences.[8] Rudolf Steiner's first Esoteric School had existed for ten years when World War I broke out, and external as well as internal difficulties emerged. The school was immensely important for Rudolf Steiner's theosophical work and for the Theosophical Society in Germany. As early as May 1, 1903, a year before it was founded, he had written in a letter that the Esoteric School would have to be the "soul" of the Theosophical Society.[9] A year later, shortly before he began with the esoteric lessons, he said again to Mathilde Scholl: "The German theosophical movement will only flourish if there is a central group of theosophists who work esoterically."[10] His early statements concur to an extent with what he said later during and after the Christmas Conference: The theosophical or anthroposophical movement relied on an "esoteric center" or spiritual "soul" that would enable it to take effect.

Rudolf Steiner did not found the Esoteric School of the Theosophical Society; it had been instituted by Helena Petrovna Blavatsky as early as 1888.[11] While Rudolf Steiner's lessons always had a distinctive quality, they belonged to that school and he devoted his esoteric work to its "masters."[12]

༄

In February 1905, just before her twenty-ninth birthday, Rudolf Steiner invited Ita Wegman to a first esoteric lesson in Berlin[13] after she had been deeply moved by a lecture he had given on Goethe's *Tale of the Green Snake and the Beautiful Lily*. The spiritual motifs of Goethe's "Michaelic miniature"[14] had formed the basis of the first esoteric lecture given by Steiner four and a half years earlier, on Michaelmas day 1900, in Berlin.[15] ("The lecture on Goethe's Tale to the core group of Berlin theosophists from which the anthroposophical movement would grow was the first interpretation of the initiation wisdom of the new Michael Age." Hella Wiesberger.[16]) Only through that theme did Ita Wegman, who was a member of the German Section of the Theosophical Society, realize Rudolf Steiner's true concern. Up to that point this had been hidden to her. Now she experienced Rudolf Steiner as an esoteric teacher. "*From that moment I knew that Rudolf Steiner was my teacher, is my teacher and will be my teacher in the future.*"[17] Unlike many other anthroposophists, Ita Wegman did not find her way to Rudolf Steiner through his lectures or writings but in her immediate experience of his esoteric teaching. She encountered Rudolf Steiner in the inner space of Anthroposophy, inside his spiritual school. ("When the word became flesh the teaching methods of the esoteric schools changed. The word had no effect in pre-Christian times. The lessons were held in silence and the pupils absorbed the communications from spiritual worlds in images.... The rightful esoteric schools of our time that have the Christ force as their center are able to teach through the word. Communication with divine-spiritual worlds used to be only possible through the sounds of the mantras. Now we can initiate the union with the Christ force inside us through words that are filled with meaning."[18])

Two years later, at Pentecost 1907, when Rudolf Steiner withdrew his school from the "Esoteric School of Theosophy" (or the "Eastern School of Theosophy"), Ita Wegman remained with him—as did most of his pupils.[19] The division was the result of serious conflicts and controversies within the Theosophical Society and brought about a "radical change" in the school's spiritual leadership.[20] The school was now Rudolf Steiner's responsibility. He dedicated it to the two "masters" of the Western Christian Rosicrucian stream and withdrew it from the influence of the Eastern "masters" that had played a prominent part until then.[21] Shortly after taking that decisive step Steiner wrote by way of explanation:

> Whether [the Theosophical Society] continues to thrive in the West depends entirely on its ability to embrace the

principle of Western initiation. Eastern initiation must necessarily ignore the *Christ principle* as the central *cosmic* factor of evolution. But without that principle the theosophical movement will not be able to govern the cultures of the West that are rooted in the life of Christ. The revelations of oriental initiation would have to stand as sects *beside* the living culture of the West. They could only hope for a successful evolution if they eradicated the Christ principle from Western culture. But that would be paramount to eradicating the *true purpose of the Earth* which is to know the intentions of the *living Christ* and putting them into action. To unveil these intentions in full wisdom, beauty, and deed is the highest endeavor of Rosicrucianism. Studying Eastern wisdom is a highly valuable enterprise because the peoples of the West have lost their understanding of esotericism, while the peoples of the East have retained theirs. The right esotericism to be *introduced* in the West must be the Rosicrucian–Christian esotericism, because it has given birth to Western life and if it was lost, humanity on Earth would repudiate its own purpose and destiny.[22]

At Pentecost 1907, immediately after the split, Rudolf Steiner asked his esoteric pupils to decide between the two schools. ("You must examine carefully where your heart directs you."[23]) At the time, Ita Wegman had a pivotal meeting with him:

> I knew it would be a crucial moment in my life. I had to decide between following the path of Rudolf Steiner wholeheartedly or remaining with the Dutch friends.
>
> He received me earnestly, a question in his eyes. We did not say much, we understood each other very well. I simply said because I felt that he knew anyway: "I will stay with you."
>
> His eyes lit up. He took my hand, gave me the Michael sign and told me important things that I am not at liberty to repeat. Ancient karma that we both shared was renewed.[24]

This is how Ita Wegman, in her notes of February 1933, described her meeting with Rudolf Steiner: the sparse conversation and his remarkable response to her decision: "*His eyes lit up. He took my hand, gave me the Michael sign and told me important things that I am not at liberty to repeat. Ancient karma that we both shared was renewed.*" Rudolf Steiner responded with a kind of ritual act: he took Ita Wegman's hand and gave her the "Michael sign." A profound esoteric dimension became tangible and, at the same time, "ancient" destiny was "*renewed*" in the age and "stream" of Michael. A few months later Rudolf Steiner spoke for the first time in an esoteric lesson of the Michael age and its beginning in 1879. To the members of his school he referred as "*disciples of Michael.*"[25] After her life-changing meeting with Rudolf Steiner of Pentecost 1907 Ita Wegman attended his esoteric lessons whenever she could get away from her studies in Zurich. In the spring of 1914, six months before the outbreak of World War II, Rudolf Steiner wrote down a mantric verse for her personal use:

> To the things I turn,
> Turn with my senses;—
> Sense being, you deceive me!—
> What flees existence as nothingness
> Is being and essence to you;
> What must seem vain to you
> May reveal itself to my soul.—
>
> Spirit light, warm me,
> Let me feel myself, as will, in you;
> Good thoughts, true knowledge,
> How I saw you radiant?
> Weaving error, evil thought,
> Reveal yourself to the radiant soul,
> That I may, weaving, be in me.

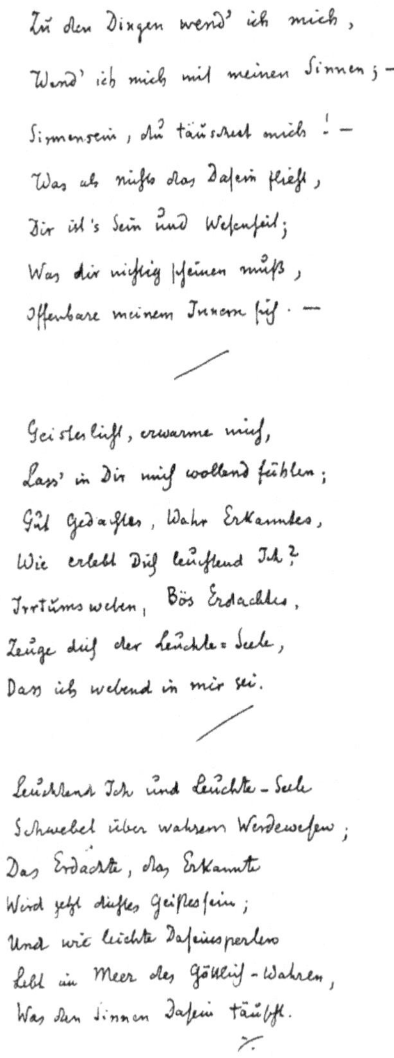

Zu den Dingen wend' ich mich,
Wend' ich mich mit meinen Sinnen; —
Sinnensein, du täuschest mich! —
Was als nichts das Dasein fließt,
Dir ist's Sein und Wesenteil;
Was dir nichtig scheinen muß,
Offenbare meinem Innern sich. —

Geisteslicht, erwarme mich,
Lass' in Dir mich wollend fühlen;
Gut Gedachtes, Wahr Erkanntes,
Wie erlebt Dich leuchtend Ich?
Irrtumsweben, Bös Erdachtes,
Zeuge dich der Leuchte-Seele,
Dass ich webend in mir sei.

Leuchtend Ich und Leuchte-Seele
Schwebet über wahrem Werdewesen;
Das Erdachte, das Erkannte
Wird jetzt dichtes Geistessein;
Und wie leichte Daseinsperlen
Lebt im Meer des Göttlich-Wahren,
Was den Sinnen Dasein täuscht.

Fig. 10: Verse, handwritten for Ita Wegman by Rudolf Steiner

> Radiant I and shining soul
> Hovering above true evolving;
> What is thought and what is known
> now condensed in spirit being;
> And like weightless pearls of being
> Lives in seas of truth divine,
> What feigns being to the senses.²⁶

Rudolf Steiner spoke about these words in three esoteric lessons in March 1914: "Each of these verses is an elaboration on what is expressed as essence in the ten words of our Rosicrucian formulae:

> *Ex Deo nascimur*
> *In Christo morimur*
> *Per Spiritum Sanctum reviviscimus.*" ²⁷

Rudolf Steiner also said:

> If we meditate on the three formulae in the right way, with feeling, the higher hierarchies will promise to help us and we can say: "We draw closer to you!" And they will reach out to us and keep their promise.²⁸

When war broke out in the summer of 1914 Rudolf Steiner discontinued his esoteric teaching. For inner as well as outer reasons he refused to resume the lessons after 1918.²⁹

༺ ༻

When Ita Wegman asked Rudolf Steiner for a "new esotericism," he had arrived at the final chapter of his life and work. The Goetheanum was destroyed. The "terrible struggle" Steiner had warned against as early as 1907 surfaced after World War II, in the early 1920s.³⁰ On the night of December 31, 1922, after ten years of building work, the intended mystery site in Dornach perished in flames. In this late, abysmal hour of total destruction the physician Ita Wegman woke up gradually to Rudolf Steiner's situation and to her role in his work due to ancient karma[31] that was renewed in 1907, in the light of the "coming Christ" or healing principle of the future. ("Since the beginning of the fifth post-Atlantean era, human life has been a gradual sickening. It is the task of education and culture to restore it to health. Healing is the first and foremost purpose of the Christ impulse. Christ has the special mission in the fifth post-Atlantean era to redeem or heal humanity. Any other aspects belonging to the Christ impulse are secondary."[32]) From 1907 onward, Rudolf Steiner had counted on the fact that Ita Wegman would awaken to her destiny. He knew about the past and the mission they shared.[33] But Ita Wegman had to undergo important and necessary developments in her biography before she was ready to discover in Rudolf Steiner her esoteric teacher.[34] "*Memory of millennia / of Mysa so lovely, gentle / of Alexander rushing and roaring / All in the bright spirit image / in present love / souls sharing their desires / these give us strength / forge arms for the soul.*"[35]

It was probably in Penmaenmawr that Wegman expressed her wish for a "new esotericism,"[36] following months of intense collaboration with Rudolf Steiner.[37] Here in Wales, the land of ancient mysteries and druids with its "elementary esoteric ambience," he was able to speak of initiation knowledge[38] in a "purely anthroposophical way" (Steiner[39]):

> One could speak differently there than in other places. There seemed to be a greater receptiveness for the spiritual world that enabled the audience, even though they had come from elsewhere, to take in the subtle stirrings reverberating from the surrounding nature and feel their way into the realm of spirit and soul. And everybody who was fortunate enough to have one or more conversations with Rudolf Steiner will have sensed something special in the atmosphere that made

those conversations special. Ancient wisdom, ancient traditions were almost tangible, as if archetypal wisdom—and many friends who were there felt this—was awakened from deep sleep by Rudolf Steiner's words. Anthroposophy seemed even more luminous. We sensed at a deeper level what we know from Anthroposophy: that the spirit weaves and lives in the physical world. We felt closer to the spirit. (Ita Wegman[40])

Rudolf Steiner was not in a position to answer Ita Wegman's question there and then ("an esoteric school cannot be created because we want it"). He conveyed the question to the spiritual world. "*The initiative for the esoteric Michael School came, as Rudolf Steiner pointed out, from Dr. Wegman*" (Polzer-Hoditz[41]). The affirmation Rudolf Steiner received from the spiritual world was a prerequisite for his founding of the Esoteric School of the Goetheanum after the Christmas Conference. Ita Wegman had asked the question in the context of the mystery lectures. On the basis of her initiative Rudolf Steiner could proceed and prepare for the future. Ita Wegman's individuality continued to be intimately associated with that future.[42] Rudolf Steiner later referred to her as his "coworker" in the Esoteric School of the Goetheanum. Ludwig Polzer-Hoditz, with whom Rudolf Steiner spoke about such matters, said in 1935, in defense of Ita Wegman:

> I think I know what Rudolf Steiner meant when he spoke of a "coworker." The appointment of a helper for the foundation and organization of a mystery institution such as the Michael School had to be based on a profound karmic relationship. Rudolf Steiner was aware of this connection and wanted to act in accordance with it.[43]

Rudolf Steiner (and the spiritual world) accepted Ita Wegman's "initiative." Polzer-Hoditz said: "*Accepting the initiative meant that the esoteric karma was created between him and her that is the prerequisite for mysteries in our times."*[44]

Rudolf Steiner began immediately after Penmaenmawr to prepare for the founding of the Michael School (also by offering an "esoteric Rosicrucian lesson" in Vienna on September 30, 1923[45]). He began to work with and train Ita Wegman spiritually. She frequently received extensive exercises from him and they meditated together and performed ritual acts that we still know little about today.[46]

Four months after Penmaenmawr, the Christmas Conference took place. It included the mantric laying of the foundation stone for the General Anthroposophical Society and the new founding of the School for Spiritual Science as an esoteric institution. Looking back in April 1925, Ita Wegman wrote: "Penmaenmawr Karma / fully revealed / soul element / understanding on my part / The spiritual world / jubilated, he said / So the next step / in the physical world was / to unite the Dr. with the / society. / A blossom was to / grow from this / even more *esotericism*, and more esotericism / mystery renewal / full revelation / of karma."[47] "*The Anthroposophical Society must grow more and more esoteric*" (Rudolf Steiner[48]).

In his evening lectures at the Christmas Conference Rudolf Steiner elaborated on the role of Anthroposophy in the history of the world and its destiny within the evolving "Michael stream."[49] Throughout the conference he gave special attention to the field of medicine.[50] With Ita Wegman and the group of young physicians around her he formed, immediately after the conference, a new academic institution of professional esotericism. Ita Wegman was his helper, in the sense described by Polzer-Hoditz. She saw it as her particular task to be his assistant.[51] With Ita Wegman, Rudolf Steiner was able to build up the medical section of the School for Spiritual Science instantly, courageously and without compromise,[52] under extremely challenging circumstances:[53]

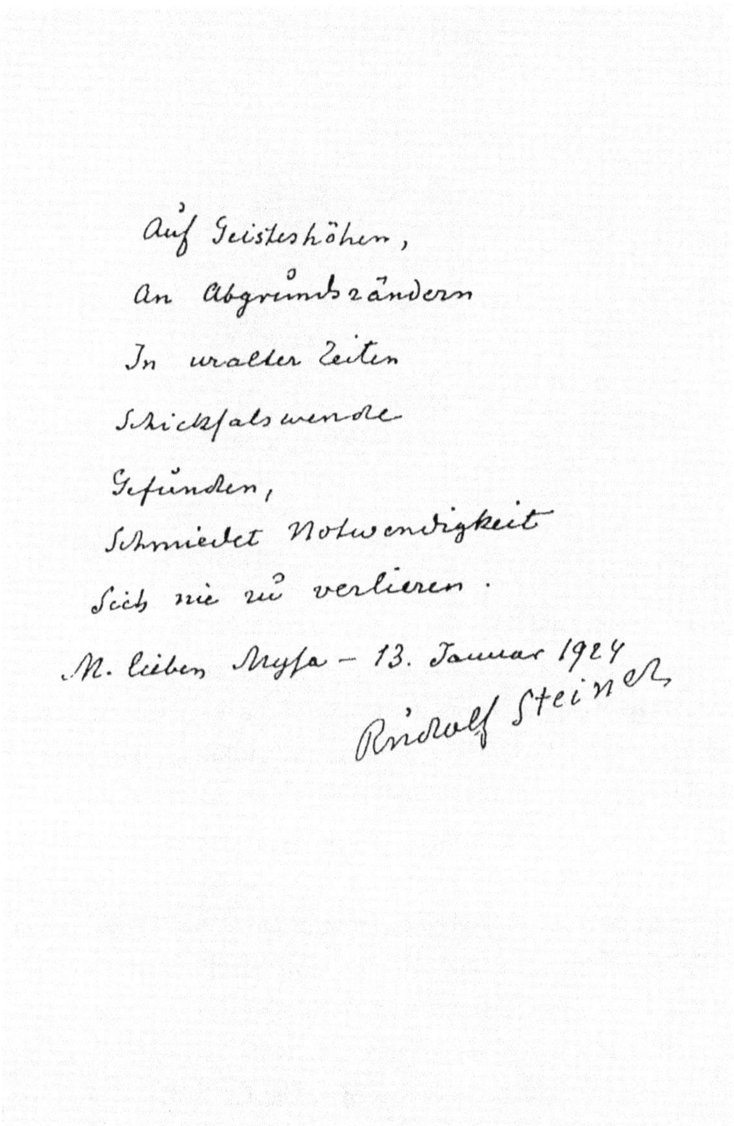

> Auf Geisteshöhen,
> An Abgrunds rändern
> In uralter Zeiten
> Schicksalswende
> Gefunden,
> Schmiedet Notwendigkeit
> Sich nie zu verlieren.
>
> M. lieben Myta — 13. Januar 1924
>
> Rudolf Steiner

Fig. 11: Rudolf Steiner: Handwritten verse for Ita Wegman, January 31, 1924

> Support I shall find
> In your understanding
> In your love and loyalty
>
> I see growing
> From your understanding
> The light that shines for me
>
> I see growing
> From your love
> The warmth that blesses me
>
> I see growing
> From your loyalty
> The air that enlivens me.[54]

೦෬

Rudolf Steiner did not speak of this to the members of the General Anthroposophical Society and School for Spiritual Science. His collaboration with Ita Wegman was part of the inner work that went on under special conditions at the center of initiation in Dornach. Rudolf Steiner had pointed out at the Christmas Conference that *"the sections are really nobody's business. The sections are formed for our work here. We need not even speak of the sections. You will find them as they need to be in order to serve their specific purposes."*[55] Steiner's unassuming words hardly touch the reality of the School for Spiritual Science that was to have, at its core, Rudolf Steiner's spiritual collaboration with the respective section leaders. Rudolf Steiner announced at the Christmas Conference that *he* would lead the sections "through" the section leaders[56] and that the inner work of the sections would remain largely invisible to members of the Society. Only their "achievements" would be made public and serve as guidelines for training.

In retrospect, we find, at least indirectly, references to Rudolf Steiner's karmic relationship and—past and present—work with Ita Wegman: in his evening lectures at the Christmas Conference, the Karma Lectures of 1924 and the important mystery cycle presented in Torquay in the summer of 1924. The Torquay lectures (*True and False Paths in Spiritual Investigation*) are essential for a deeper understanding of the School for Spiritual Science, its *raison d'être* and spiritual orientation.[57] Based on what he communicated in Torquay (even though it was not fully understood) and because he felt that it was urgently necessary for members to wake up, Rudolf Steiner was, from the end of summer 1924, able (if not obliged) to speak openly about the new Esoteric School's Michaelic dimension—and about Ita Wegman's involvement in that school. "*He said to me [in August 1924] that it was time for people to know that the Class was the Michael School in the spiritual world. That he was the leader of that school and I his assistant. It was my task to guard the mantras. Any member who wanted to pass the mantras on to another member had to consult either him or me. This was an esoteric act, the beginning of an esotericism that was to be newly initiated. Newly admitted members would hear the words: This is the Michael School that is led by me and Dr. Wegman.*"[58] From the late summer of 1924 Rudolf Steiner introduced ritual elements to the class lessons (the "Signs and Seals of Michael"). From September onward he mentioned Ita Wegman explicitly in every lesson (in relation to the passing on of mantras through the class leaders) and began to perform a short admission for new members of the School for Spiritual Science:[59]

> Admittance took place in the studio. I had to stand beside the Doctor, members were guided into the studio by Dr. Wachsmuth. Dr. Steiner addressed a few questions to the person to be admitted and if there was nothing to prevent admittance he would speak the following words: "*If you want to remain loyal to*

the Michael School, take my hand and also the hand of Dr. Wegman who will lead the Michael School with me.[60]

The intense admission ritual in the ambience of Rudolf Steiner's studio, the space where he worked on the Christ statue, belonged to the inner work of the Class or School for Spiritual Science. "Members will hardly have forgotten the mood that prevailed during admissions," Ita Wegman would later write to Albert Steffen.[61] Seventeen years earlier, when she decided to remain with Rudolf Steiner's Esoteric School, he also took Ita Wegman's hand and gave her the "Michael sign." "I will stay with you." Now he continued with her on the path of Michael. "*Mysa stands under Mikael / transfigured*," he wrote above a sign in the summer of 1924, shortly before departing for Torquay, his last journey abroad.[62]

In his studio, under Ita Wegman's medical regime and care, their esoteric work carried on day after day throughout his illness. ("*Christian Rosenkreutz played an important part in these meditations.*"[63]) Rudolf Steiner gave Ita Wegman a rose cross he used to wear himself. As long as she lived that cross represented the First Class for her:

> Before his illness the Doctor gave me a small cross with small rubies set in roses that he used to wear on a red ribbon around his neck. He put it on me with his own hands after we had performed a ritual act.[64]

Fig. 12: Reverse of Rudolf Steiner's rose cross

4.

The Ritual Act and the Rose Cross

"Benedictus deus qui dedit nobis signum"

> "*From this moment we will both be there for the Michael School.*"
> —RUDOLF STEINER TO ITA WEGMAN

When, five months after Rudolf Steiner's death on August 21, 1925, Ita Wegman wrote to Albert Steffen about her relationship with the First Class of the School for Spiritual Science, she mentioned a rose cross given to her by Rudolf Steiner: "Before his illness the Doctor gave me a small cross with small rubies set in roses that he used to wear on a red ribbon around his neck. He put it on me with his own hands after we had performed a ritual act."[1] Rudolf Steiner's rose cross can be found as part of Ita Wegman's estate.[2] A few years later, on April 25, 1930, Ita Wegman spoke about the circumstances of the handing over of the cross, the preceding "ritual act" and their connection with the First Class during an Executive Council meeting with the general secretaries and delegates of the General Anthroposophical Society at the Goetheanum: "I also received his cross directly. He took it from his neck and put it on me with his own hands, saying: '*From this moment we will be there together for the Michael School.*'"[3]

This meant that Rudolf Steiner, after performing the ritual act and through the ritual of handing over the cross, admitted Ita Wegman to the Michael School as coleader with joint responsibility. It is not known when the event took place. Ita Wegman mentioned no date, but she wrote to Albert Steffen that it was "before" Rudolf Steiner's illness, which first became apparent in late September 1924. There is sufficient reason to believe that Rudolf Steiner performed the ritual act and the passing on of the cross at the beginning of September 1924 (after his return from England) in his studio. In all class lessons held by him from September 6 onward he emphasized Ita Wegman's special joint responsibility for the mantras of the ritual lessons and for the Esoteric School.[4] People who were admitted to the First Class in September 1924 were ritually introduced by Steiner and Wegman together. "Admittance took place in the studio. I had to stand beside the Doctor, members were guided into the studio by Dr. Wachsmuth. Dr. Steiner addressed a few questions to the person to be admitted and if there was nothing to prevent admittance he would speak the following words: *If you want to remain loyal to the Michael School, take my hand and also the hand of Dr. Wegman who will lead the Michael School with me*" (Ita Wegman[5]). Among the class members who were admitted in September 1924 was Wolfgang Moldenhauer, who described the admission procedure in the exact same way in a letter to Kurt Franz David: "On September 5, 1924, I was admitted to the First Class by Rudolf Steiner. After the handshake that was a pledge of loyalty at the same time he asked me to take the hand of Dr. Wegman, his coleader, who was sitting next to him."[6] In notes she took for an internal lecture Ita Wegman wrote a brief summary about the changes in the affairs of the First Class in late summer 1924: "He said to me [in August 1924] that it was time for people to know that the Class was the Michael School in the spiritual world. That he was the leader of that school and I his assistant. It was my task to guard the mantras. Any member who wanted to pass the mantras on to another member had to consult either him or me. This was an esoteric act, the beginning of an esotericism that was to be newly initiated. Newly admitted members would hear the words: *This is the Michael School that is led by me and Dr. Wegman.*"[7]

Nothing further has so far been discovered about the handing over of the rose cross and especially about the preceding ritual act, although both—obviously associated—procedures were highly significant also for the class lessons, since from that time the first ritual elements (the "signs and seal of Michael") were introduced to the lessons. The unpublished minutes of an Executive Council meeting of November 29, 1930, reveal that a document about the performed ritual act was in Ita Wegman's possession. When, during the crisis of the Executive Council and the Society, Ita Wegman was forced again to confirm to her colleagues that Rudolf Steiner had indeed conferred joint responsibility for the Class on her (nobody apart from Elisabeth Vreede believed her), she spoke about the ritual act: "[Tomorrow] I will take [bring] along the papers where he [Dr. Steiner] actually said it to me. I will read out the act where he said it."[8] Whether Ita Wegman actually went on to do that on November 30, 1930, is not documented.

Ita Wegman spoke of the joint performance of a ritual act that was sealed with the handing over of the rose cross. The "papers" recording the ritual act or aspects of that act form part of a comprehensive collection of mantras and esoteric exercises in Rudolf Steiner's handwriting that she had received from him. The collection is preserved in full and was published in 2009 by the priest Emanuel Zeylmans van Emmichoven.[9] It includes a text covering several sheets in Rudolf Steiner's and Ita Wegman's hands. The text focuses on the rose cross and its handing over, culminating in the handing over, and contains ritual elements of a ritual antiphony between two people. Emanuel Zeylmans van Emmichoven wrote: "Because Ita Wegman wrote down Rudolf Steiner's oral instructions it is possible for us to place the text right into its individual images and personal statements before our soul."[10] Considering all that is known about the context, there is little doubt that those sheets reflect or contain the ritual act performed by Rudolf Steiner with Ita Wegman in late summer 1924.[11] The text includes an evening and a morning meditation for Ita Wegman, both culminating in the meeting with a priest figure and the handing over of a rose cross. The mantric verses are associated with the esoteric training of the First Class and end with a blessing on the meditating person who receives the rose cross from the priest figure—the *"spirit guide."* How much of the text was spoken in the performance of the act in Rudolf Steiner's studio can only be guessed, but one can assume that at least the antiphonal words about the rose cross and the concluding ritual blessing were enunciated.

༄

The evening meditation exercise for Ita Wegman begins with the review of one of the day's experiences ("imagine an experience of the day in reverse order"[12]). This is followed by exact instructions by Rudolf Steiner, taken down in her handwriting, of a breathing exercise that is to be repeated seven times, an IAO exercise, then the "Rose Cross imagination." The imagination was obviously meant to be linked to a mantra referring to the spiritual human form and was to be meditated in relation to that form (focusing on heart and limb organization[13]):

> Primal Powers hold me
> Spirits of fire free me
> Spirits of light illumine me
> So that I reach toward spirit life
> So that I feel beings of soul
> So that I traverse uncertainties
> So that I stand above the abyss.[14]

If meditated accordingly, the Rose Cross imagination will convey strength and support to the human being from the third hierarchy (in the region of the heart) so that inner certainty can be gained for meeting the tasks and dangers of humanity with confidence.

That process of strengthening, affirmation and empowerment (or encouragement) was to be followed by further deepened concentration—full inner immersion into the Christ Mystery with the mantra:

> In me let Christ live
> And change my breath
> And warm the course of my blood
> And shine into my soul being.[15]

Rudolf Steiner's transcript of the evening meditation ends with the instruction: "Maintain inner poise." In the margin of the page Steiner had added behind a square bracket: "White robe. Red belt and pendant. Red headband. I: *Ave frater.* He: *Rosae et aureae.* I: Crucis. He: *Benedictus deus qui dedit nobis signum.*"

What Steiner had written down and passed on to Ita Wegman was obviously a summary that served as a reminder. He would have specified the inner process to her in much more detail verbally. According to Wegman's notes, the "Rose Cross" had to be retrieved from the heart of the meditating person, where it had previously been "placed" after the Christ meditation. Wegman did not specify in her notes whether the Rose Cross meditation—on the mantric verse "Primal Powers hold me"—was to be experienced as the spiritual *configuration* of a rose cross (and its retention in the heart as the central human organ). The overall movement seems to indicate however that the rose cross had to be created, or reproduced, mantrically and internalized during the exercise.

After the rose cross had been "retrieved" from the heart it had to be carried imaginatively up a mountain, "step by step." On the mountain peak an encounter should take place in the imagination with a figure ("person") in priestly ritual vestment (with white robe, red stole, red band around the neck and red belt, the colors of Christian Rosenkreutz—white and red—in the *Chymical Wedding*.) Ita Wegman wrote about that meeting:

> One has to hand the rose cross over to that person with the words *"Ave frater"* [Hail thee, brother], and sense the other's response: *"Rosae and aureae"* [of the rosy and golden]. With devotion one answers: *"Crucis"* [cross]. The other speaks: *"Benedictus deus qui dedit nobis signum"* [Blessed be God who gave us the sign].

After the imaginative experience of such a meeting, that is, the joint—*antiphonal*—enunciation of the words: "Hail thee, brother of the rosy and golden cross," the blessing of God through the priestly figure and the handing over to that figure of the rose cross that has been carried up, the meditating person turns back. "Then the imagination that one leaves the other again. After that, allow a sense of calm to enter into the soul. Empty the mind." The rose cross remains on the mountain.

ତ୍ତ

As a reminder for the morning meditation Rudolf Steiner wrote merely:

> Imagination on the mountain. Being received.
> Holding up [the rose cross]
>
> May my head condense the spirit of worlds
> Extracting for me the living light of thoughts
> May my throat parch the breath of soul
> Infusing it with spirit word meaning
> Inhabit my *heart*, you, my spirit guide
> There to unite me with you
> That I move live weave in spirit soul life.

Ita Wegman added more details to her notes:

> Imagine in the morning:
> That one has climbed up the mountain again, that one meets the same person in the same robe; that the figure gives back the rose cross given to him [her] on the previous evening.
>
> Imagination to be meditated, kneeling down:
>
> > 1. May my head condense the spirit of worlds
> > Extracting for me the living light of thoughts
> > 2. May my throat parch the breath of soul
> > Infusing it with spirit word meaning
> > 3. Inhabit my *heart*, you, my spirit guide
> > There to unite me with you
> > That I move live weave in spirit soul life!
>
> > Feel the head—the thinking—like a stone
> > The throat like a parched plant
> > Concentration on the heart while meditating the above.
>
> Now meditate that the person gives back the rose cross, that he places the right hand on top of the left, then both hands on the forehead, speaking the words:
>
> > "Benedictus deus qui dedit nobis signum"
>
> Empty the mind again.

The meditation of the pupil climbing the mountain again, which is carried out while kneeling, culminates in the spiritual union with the priestly figure in the heart, the human organ of destiny. (*"Inhabit my heart, you, my spirit guide, there to unite me with you"*). After that, as Ita Wegman's notes suggest, the "spirit guide" gives [returns] the rose cross to the pupil, with a blessing and laying of hands on the pupil's forehead.

"And I... received his cross directly. He took it from his neck and put it on me with his own hands, saying: '*From this moment we will be there together for the Michael School.'"* With those worlds Ita Wegman described how Rudolf Steiner handed over the cross to her directly after performing the ritual act. "In united soul effort,"[16] united in the spirit ("there to unite me with you"), Rudolf Steiner wanted to work actively for the Michael School with Ita Wegman, accompanying and supporting her on her inner path, but also needing her assistance.[17]

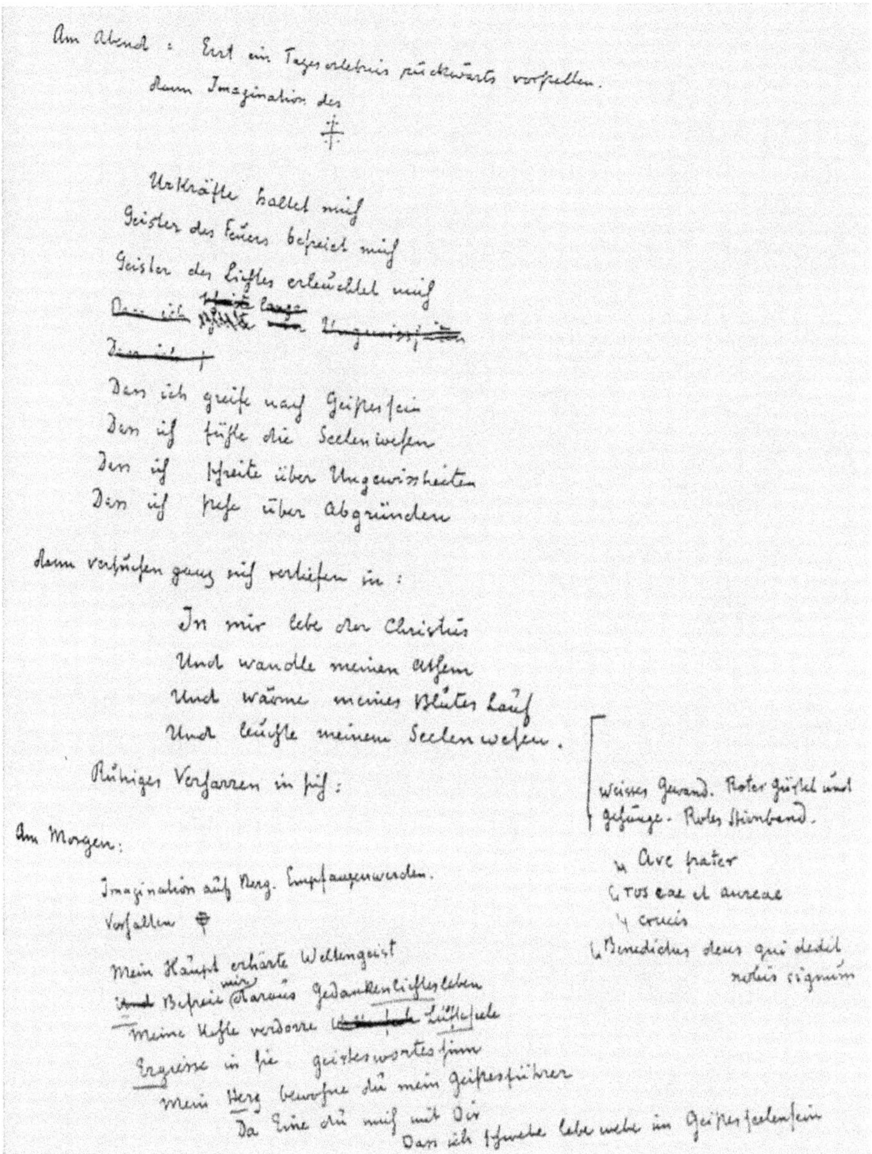
Am Abend: Erst ein Tageserlebnis rückwärts vorstellen.
dann Imagination des
Urkräfte hallet mich
Geister des Feuers befreiet mich
Geister des Lichtes erleuchtet mich
Dass ich greife nach Geistessein
Dass ich fühle die Seelenwesen
Dass ich schreite über Ungewissheiten
Dass ich stehe über Abgründen
dann versuchen ganz sich vertiefen in:
In mir lebe der Christus
Und wandle meinen Athem
Und wärme meines Blutes Lauf
Und leuchte meinem Seelenwesen.
Ruhiges Verharren in sich:
Am Morgen:
Imagination auf Herz. Empfangenwerden.
Vorstellen
Mein Haupt erhärte Weltengeist
Befreie mir daraus Gedankenlichtesleben
Meine Kehle verdorre Lichtesseele
Ergiesse in sie Geisteswortes Sinn
Mein Herz bewahre du mein Geistesführer
Da eine du mich mit Dir
Dass ich schwebe lebe webe in Geistesseelensein
Weisses Gewand. Roter Gürtel und Gehänge. Rotes Stirnband.
Ave frater
Rosae et aureae
crucis
Benedictus deus qui dedit nobis signum

Fig. 13: Rudolf Steiner's handwritten notes for meditations

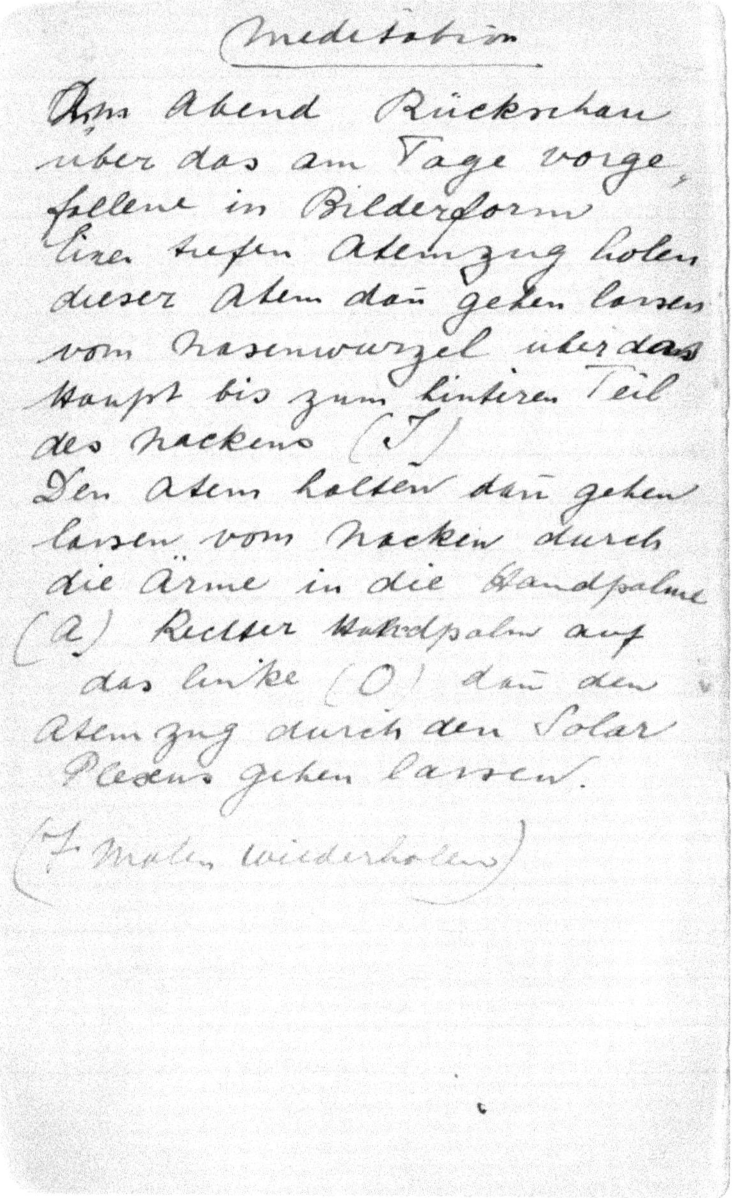

Meditation

Am Abend Rückschau
über das am Tage vorge-
fallene in Bilderform
Einen tiefen Atemzug holen
dieser Atem dann gehen lassen
vom Nasenwurzel über das
Haupt bis zum hinteren Teil
des Nackens (J)
Den Atem halten dann gehen
lassen vom Nacken durch
die Arme in die Handpalme
(a) Rechter Handpalm auf
das linke (O) dann den
Atemzug durch den Solar
Plexus gehen lassen.
(7 Mal wiederholen)

Fig. 14: Ita Wegman's handwriting (above and following pages):
notes for meditations

The Ritual Act and the Rose Cross

```
                    1
(geller)       3 0 ⚹ 0 2    (linker)
 linker        ─────┼─────  rechter Handpalm
 Handpalm      4 0  │ 0 5
                    0   0
 rechtes       7    │ 6.   linkes Bein
 Bein
```

1-2-3
Herz   1) Urkräfte haltet mich
aroha 2) Geister des Feuers befreiet mich
anglo 3) Geister des Lichts erleuchtet mich
       4) Dass ich greife noch
                        Geisteswesen
       5) Dass ich fühle die Seelenwesen
       6) Dass ich schreite über Länge,
                   wir leiten
       7) Dass ich stehe über Abgründen

       ―

Dan meditieren die Worte
    In mir lebe der Christus
Und wandle meinen Atem
Und leuchte meinen Seelenwesen

Nach dieser Meditation das

Rosenkreuz aus dem Herzen
in dem man es vorher gelegt
hat herausholen
Daraufhin muss man die
Imagination haben dass
man Schritt für Schritt
einen Berg hinaufsteigt
den Rosenkreuz tragend.
Auf der Bergspitze begegnet
man eine Person in einem
weissen Gewand mit roter
Stola, rotem Gurt und rotem
Band um dem Hals
An dieser Person gibt man
den Rosenkreuz und sagt
zu ihm „Ave frater"
Man fühlt, dass der andere
antwortet „Rosae et aurae
man antwortet mit devotion
zurück. Crucis"
Der andere sagt: „Benedictus
Deus qui dedit nobis signum
qui

Dann die weitere Imagination
dass man diesen andern
verläßt
Daraufhin Ruhe eintreten
lassen in der Seele
Leer machen das Bewußtsein

—

Morgens imaginieren:
dass man wieder den Berg
aufgestiegen ist, dass man
die gleiche Person mit der
gleichen Gewandung begegnet
und dass diese das Rosen-
kreuz wieder zurückgibt
das man ihm den vorigen
Abend gegeben hat
Imaginieren, dass man
knieend das folgende meditiert:
1) Mein Haupt erhärte Weltengeist
Befreie mir daraus Gedankenhelleslebe[n]
2) Meine Kehle verdorre Lüfteseele
Ergiesse in die Geisteswortesinn
3) Mein Herz bewohne du mein Geistesfüh[len]
Da eine Du mich mit Dir
Dass ich schwebe lebe webe in Geistesseelensein

1) Fühlen das Haupt (wie ein der denken Stein.
2) Die Kehle wie eine verdorrte Pflanze
3) Concentration auf das Herz bei der meditation des vorangegangenen

—

Nun ist zu meditieren dass diese Person den Rosenkreuz zurückgibt; dass er die rechte Hand auf die linke legt, dann beide Hände auf die Stirn legt und die folgenden Worte spricht:
„Benedictus Deus qui dedit nobis signum."
wieder leeres Bewustsein machen

Fig. 15: Rudolf Steiner and Ita Wegman, Arnhem, July 1924

5.

Ita Wegman Holds the Class Lessons

"I am inwardly committed to this Michael School. I will be guided by this commitment and take responsibility in my actions."

—Ita Wegman[1]

"Since the Doctor said and continued to repeat that the Michael School was instituted by the spiritual world and that it was not a human institution, I felt I was appointed by the spiritual world and had no right, after his death, to introduce any changes. I only asked myself: can I, as the second leader, after the first, and main leader was no longer able to lead the school in person, watch over the school and continue to direct it while making sure that the wisdom of the Michael School as given by Dr. Steiner in the class lessons is maintained? I said inwardly 'yes' to this question."
—Ita Wegman [2]

After Rudolf Steiner's death on March 30, 1925, it was difficult for Ita Wegman to continue with the "First Class." In the Easter Program of the Goetheanum, which was published a few weeks later, she found no class lessons advertised—and she was not asked for his program at all. Her colleagues in the Executive Council were not even sure about the position and tasks she had within the Esoteric School.[3]

Ita Wegman saw no alternative to continuing on the path that had begun with the Christmas Conference. She saw this path as Rudolf's intention and legacy. She wrote essays about the important contents of the karma lectures—especially in relation to the "Michael mystery"—to make them more accessible to all members of the Anthroposophical Society.[4] It was her intention to hold class lessons in many places: "*We knew that, for the time being, it was a matter of guarding the esoteric contents that had been given and of bringing to life in the members the powers inherent in this esotericism.*"[5]

It was never Ita Wegman's intention to "read out" the words given by Rudolf Steiner out of reverence for the past. By repeating those words she wanted to "bring to life in the members the powers inherent in this esotericism." She wanted to "disseminate" the First Class—as a "Michael School and continuation of Michael's suprasensory teachings"[6]—in the way Rudolf Steiner had given it. Beginning with the first lesson she wanted to win understanding for the First Class[7] by presenting it to a small group of members so that the "the intimate character of the lessons"[8] would be retained. It was Ita Wegman's endeavor to do this in many different countries. After difficult discussions in the Executive Council[9] she began in Paris on May 25, 1925, eight weeks after Rudolf Steiner's death. She wanted to let "Michael's words resound" everywhere so that they could take effect in his disciples[10] as befitted the cosmopolitan nature of the Michael Age. We do not know whether she had ever discussed such steps with Rudolf Steiner who himself had held class lessons in Paris, Prague, Wroclaw, Arnhem, Torquay and London. It is unlikely since she never referred to any such conversation. But it is also true that "the intentions of Dr. Steiner"[11] were all that counted for Ita Wegman and one must therefore assume that many confidential conversations about the Class had taken place between them. ("I heard much about this school from Rudolf Steiner and about the relationship he and I have with it."[12])

༺༻

In the class lessons she began to hold soon after March 30, 1925, in Vienna, Prague and London, Ita Wegman usually gave an introduction with comments on how the class should be dealt with and her own approach to it. She would then read the lessons in Rudolf Steiner's words that had been taken down in shorthand by Helene Finkh with his consent. She said about these

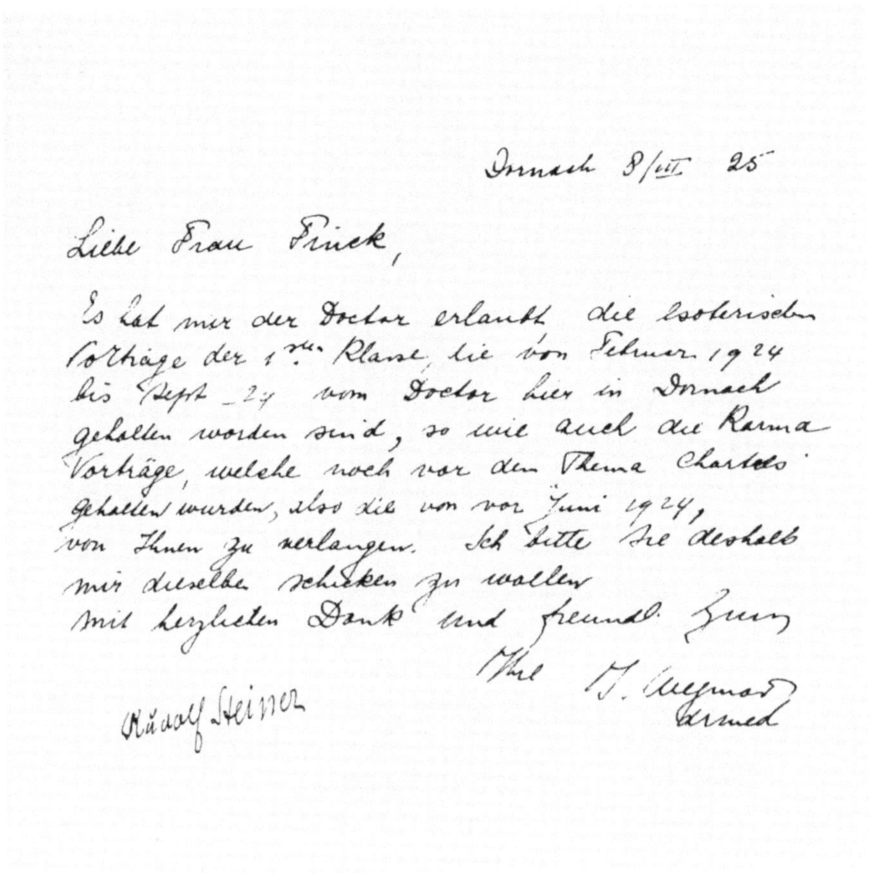

Dornach 8/III 25

Liebe Frau Finck,

Es hat mir der Doctor erlaubt die Esoterischen Vorträge der 1ten Klasse, die von Februar 1924 bis Sept. 24 vom Doctor hier in Dornach gehalten worden sind, so wie auch die Karma Vorträge, welche noch vor dem Thema Chartres gehalten wurden, also die von vor Juni 1924, von Ihnen zu verlangen. Ich bitte Sie deshalb mir dieselben schicken zu wollen

Mit herzlichen Dank und freundl. Gruss

Ihre I. Wegman

Rudolf Steiner

Fig. 16: Rudolf Steiner/Ita Wegman:
Letter to Helene Finkch, March 8, 1925

words that "*they can only be read out, my dear friends, because in this way Michael words are repeated to you unmodified, as Dr. Steiner spoke them.*"[13] Ita Wegman had transcripts of all nineteen lessons. She had received them with Rudolf Steiner's explicit permission at the time of his illness. ("The doctor always pointed out . . . that shorthand notes of the class lessons did not really exist and if one was to read from them this would have to happen with due circumspection and responsibility. He gave me the task to study the Michael School intensely and when I said that I did not have the shorthand notes he allowed me to ask Mrs. Finkh about them. He even signed the letter I wrote to Mrs. Finkh, the official stenotypist."[14]) Ita Wegman knew that Rudolf Steiner had permitted no one but Lilly Kolisko to read the transcriptions of the lessons in Stuttgart. For her there was a difference between holding lessons in that way and reading the mantras and commenting on them freely. She would speak of esoteric "class lessons" only if Rudolf Steiner's exact words were read out, if his words were resurrected in the souls of the members, if the words that had become written letters were re-enlivened. Before a class lesson in Paris she said:

> A law was broken here for the first time when esoteric contents were written down. It never happened, not in ancient times either, that esoteric contents were written down. Esoteric knowledge was only ever passed on orally.
>
> We must be well aware of this and approach the class lessons with great warmth and enthusiasm, to bring back to life what is written down here, as it was when it flowed to us from the lips of the great Master. I appeal to your warmth of heart, to your full enthusiasm, that you approach this lesson in the right way and with the right inner attitude."[15]

Rudolf Steiner had spoken repeatedly of the *"heart understanding"* that was necessary for absorbing the contents of the esoteric lessons,[16] the necessary warmth and *"deep inner feeling."*[17] Ita Wegman, who referred to herself as "Rudolf Steiner's coworker in the school," also emphasized the importance of the relevant qualities. She could not but follow faithfully the exact words Rudolf Steiner had said to her. They made her feel intimately connected and committed to the "Michael School." (*"The Michael School as an institution of the spiritual world, the words* of Rudolf Steiner, I had to take seriously, since I see the spiritual world and the laws that stream from it as realities."[18]) Despite the difficulties and controversies that arose in the Anthroposophical Society, Ita Wegman continued to hold the class lessons in this sense, in memory of Rudolf Steiner and of what she had experienced with him and in him:

> And so I would like to stand before you, dear friends, and repeat Rudolf Steiner's words, carry forward his love and loyalty to you to the best of my ability.[19]

Ita Wegman wanted to carry forward Rudolf Steiner's "love" and "loyalty" to his esoteric pupils, to the members of the School for Spiritual Science; his connection to them and their connection to him. She wanted to maintain what Polzer-Hoditz described as the "esoteric connection" to the spirit teacher whose "helper" she was in the Esoteric School.

༄

In the years from 1925 up to 1934, when serious illness brought her close to death, Ita Wegman stood firmly by her intentions although she had many other tasks and despite the escalating conflict within the General Anthroposophical Society. Ita Wegman read the class lessons at anthroposophic work meetings in various countries and when she visited the curative education centers where she served as mentor. The class lessons with their focus on Rudolf Steiner and the essence of Anthroposophy were important in those centers, for the individuals working there but also as a way of esoteric community building in very challenging times.[20] On February 12, 1933, the curative teacher Werner Pache wrote to Ita Wegman from the Institute for Curative Education in Hamborn:

We would ask again if you could arrange a visit to Hamborn on your way back from England, so that you can hold a class lesson here. Standing on Wittenberg Square in Berlin the day before yesterday, where—as in many public places—Hitler's speech was heard blaring from the loudspeakers and Ahriman's power seemed unbounded, I suddenly felt a great sense of calm and confidence. The feeling was so strong that I was torn away from the power of this evil force; a feeling that our cause will not perish.[21]

Rudolf Steiner had, in the class lessons, spoken of the forthcoming struggle with the powers of darkness and evil and of the necessity to develop inner forces for overcoming them. With the beginning of Adolf Hitler's regime in Germany in 1933 came the permission to "destroy life that was not worth living." Werner Pache worked in a home for "disabled children." These children needed to be protected and saved from such policies and this was ultimately achieved with Ita Wegman's support.[22] The First Class lessons provided substance and spiritual support that were of immeasurable importance regardless of the difficulties and problems in Dornach. In the midst of the Nazi euphoria that heralded abysmal developments, Werner Pache thought of Ita Wegman and the esoteric lessons. ("I suddenly felt a great sense of calm and confidence. The feeling was so strong that I was torn away from the power of that evil force; a feeling that our cause will not perish.") *Through* the lessons Werner Pache was brought close to Steiner and his great individuality that continued to be active. "Tell the friends in Berlin... *then I will be with you!*" (Rudolf Steiner[23]).

༄

The illness she succumbed to in February 1934, when she was 58 years old, tore Ita Wegman away from her tasks and from the conflicts.[24] For a long time she felt the wish to die, convinced that she had accomplished her task on Earth. She had been denounced in the main auditorium of the Goetheanum as the "carcinoma of the Anthroposophical Society" and was facing exclusion from the Executive Council and the Section.[25] Then she had a profound, spiritual Christ experience. At a crucial moment of her biography she encountered the Christ being (and Rudolf Steiner) in the spiritual–etheric world and regained her life forces and her strong commitment to the future. *"The experience in the spiritual world told me...something different [other than death]. During an encounter I had with Rudolf Steiner, where the Christ being was also present, I learned that I was not expected in the spiritual world—but I still had things to do on Earth. From that moment my strength returned and I was able to take my recovery strongly into my own hands."*[26]

While convalescing, Ita Wegman traveled to Palestine. There she studied the landscape and the spirituality of the events surrounding the life of Christ at the turning point of time, including the insights Rudolf Steiner first presented in his lectures on the "Fifth Gospel."[27] Rudolf Steiner had planned this journey with Ita Wegman during his illness. Now she embarked on it alone, eighteen months after the Nazis had seized power in Germany and, with full awareness of the struggles surrounding Christ's being, influence and etheric reappearance, which was not only overshadowed, but also endangered by the political reality. Rudolf Steiner's lectures on the "Fifth Gospel," as well as his creation of the "Representative of Humanity" as the "crowning" of the building in Dornach concerned this—endangered—future. Ita Wegman knew this only too well.[28] During her prolonged absence from Dornach and Arlesheim she reflected profoundly on the situation of Anthroposophy. Her near-death experience and meeting with the Christ had enhanced her recollection of the "I" impulse in her earthly biography, of what was essential for her own path, her tasks and aims. After her late return to Arlesheim, Ita Wegman wrote on February 22, 1935, her fifty-ninth birthday, to Maria Röschl, looking back over the past months and her experiences:

> While I was far away from Dornach I always felt certain that I had to remain unperturbed by everything and faithful in my heart to Rudolf Steiner's intentions, to what he intended to bring into the world with the Christmas Conference; and that I should not give in to the illusion that I had to grieve over something that could not be done, and keep grieving and do nothing, but that I should make a decision that would enable me to work.
>
> And so it became clear to me one day that I had to go back to Rudolf Steiner's original impulse; the impulse he wanted to give to the new Society by bringing down—even more strongly than before—from the association of the spirit (the Michaelic school) in the spiritual world what Michael teaches there. I heard much about this school from Rudolf Steiner, and about the relationship he and I have with it. I want to return to the original impulse that formed the essence of the Christmas Conference. I want to connect myself strongly with that impulse and act out of it. I can't say yet what will come of it. I will prepare myself and wait and I will neither push myself to the fore nor will I bind myself. If there is something good in this impulse and if people can be found who can be enthusiastic about it then something will come of it. The impulse holds a seed for the future, the last gift Rudolf Steiner entrusted to us on Earth. What was given as the First Class and is now in the hands of many, is not exhausted yet but needs to be treated in a different way. As I move on cautiously matters grow clearer. All the old forms, also the very last form for Anthroposophy, have been thoroughly destroyed. I have the impression now that we no longer need to search for a form for Anthroposophy to live in, but each individual person is a form that Anthroposophy wants to unite with. Where this has happened people will

find each other and unite as members of the true association of the spirit. The society is no longer needed, because Anthroposophy has arrived on Earth. It is now up to individuals to develop themselves and form a higher association that is rooted in the spiritual world. Individual development, the freedom of each individual, is therefore safeguarded. And people will, out of their own insight, feel connected with this association of the spirit or the Michael School. I felt this deeply. What is important is that I stand firmly in this impulse. Then everything else will fall into place.[29]

As soon as she was back in Arlesheim in November 1934—four months before her letter to Maria Röschl—Ita Wegman informed close friends and companions that the First Class would in future be at the center of her work (*"She would like to make this her most important concern."* [Willem Zeylmans van Emmichoven][30]), in order to return to the "original impulse" of the Christmas Conference:

> My task is clear: I have to gather people around me who still have a true connection with the Christmas Conference. There might not be many but I am convinced that, if this does not happen, something spiritual and precious will perish; a spiritual stream that I have to guard and that I want to carry over in its purity.[31]

Ita Wegman expressed a deep wish to "do only what relates directly to Michael; only what is impulse from the Christmas Conference:"

> One cannot speak much about this. I want to hold it in my heart and try to feel myself connected with the spiritual association in the spiritual world, because the mirror image of the spiritual association, the Anthroposophical Society, can no longer form the chalice for what can stream from this association of the spirit. Slowly, very slowly we must build up the

chalice again, let it grow again, purely. Maybe that can only happen in people's hearts.³²

After her serious illness and her meeting with the spiritual Christ, Ita Wegman wanted to rebuild the "chalice" of the anthroposophic community—"*slowly, very slowly*"—out of the Michael School and in accordance with Rudolf Steiner's intention of 1923/24, knowing now that the process would need time and that it would primarily take place in people's hearts. She was determined at least to give a chance to this building process that was connected with the Christmas Conference and relied on the social reality of esotericism. ("If a few people could bestir themselves and participate in their hearts in what I see as the original impulse of the Christmas Conference, there might be a chance of things becoming better again. If not, it is still my task to carry in my heart what Rudolf Steiner wanted and take it back to the spiritual world."³³) Ita Wegman knew better than anybody else what Rudolf Steiner had intended with the Christmas Conference and the School for Spiritual Science. She had been closely involved in their shaping and development, a fact that not many people were aware of in 1935. Ita Wegman wanted to go back to the "original impulse" of the Christmas Conference and the esoteric foundation at the Goetheanum as the School of Michael, brought to Earth by Rudolf Steiner. "*I have heard much of this school from Rudolf Steiner, and about the relationship he and I have with it.*" The continuation of Michael's heavenly instruction on Earth was for Ita Wegman the essential "seed for the future" of Anthroposophy and the "last gift Rudolf Steiner had entrusted to people on Earth." Ita Wegman wanted to start right there after life had been restored to her. But she wanted to do it differently. She had decided "I will not push myself to the fore nor will I bind myself." The letter, Ita Wegman wrote to Maria Röschl early in

1935, reveals that she questioned the Anthroposophical Society's raison d'être and significance. Too much had happened and too much had been destroyed, but she also realized that the impulse of the Michael School did not need a society, but could be found in each individual human I. ("The society is no longer needed, because Anthroposophy has arrived on Earth. It is now up to individuals to develop themselves and form a higher association that is rooted in the spiritual world.")

When putting her insights into practice, Ita Wegman made every effort to keep the First Class—*"as an entirely neutral spiritual gift"*[34]—away from the crisis-ridden Society. She wanted to guard it and lead it to the future *"free from any bonds with the Anthroposophical Society."*[35] Following the years of conflict Ita Wegman felt no longer responsible for the General Anthroposophical Society and the Goetheanum. Her commitment was to the First Class since Rudolf Steiner had explicitly connected her with it. ("To this Michael School I am inwardly committed. I will be guided in my actions by this commitment and take responsibility. I want to reawaken awareness of this spirit association that exists in the spiritual world."[36]) She wanted to make a fresh start and lead the Esoteric School into the future without any attachments to the Society, its problems and claims, also with regard to her own person. At a meeting on January 27, 1935, that Ita Wegman had convened, Werner Pache briefly noted what she said:

> About the spirit association and the Christmas Conference, to live this very faithfully. She wanted this herself. Finally, decision to hold class lessons again, freely. Beginning made.[37]

That Ita Wegman held the class lessons "freely" meant that they were wholly detached from the difficulties in Dornach. It did not mean that she worked without Rudolf Steiner's original texts as happens in the "free renderings" we know today.[38] Marianne Fiechter-Bischof, who heard all of Ita Wegman's class lessons between August 1937 and December 1942 in Arlesheim, gave a description of those gatherings.[39] On the day of the class lesson one would never see Ita Wegman at the clinic, not even at mealtimes. When she read the lessons she would wear a black robe that Rudolf Steiner had recommended. She would read in a calm and entirely objective voice, fully immersed in the rhythm of Rudolf Steiner's language. Her reading was fluent and selfless; her voice medium-pitched, natural and simple. Her figure was surrounded by the strongly esoteric atmosphere that was created through the lesson. During her lifetime there were never any conversations about the lesson contents or the mantras in Arlesheim. After the lessons she tended to disappear as she had come: without pretension and with a firm and resolute step. She only ever spoke Rudolf Steiner's words, "responsibly" and "carefully," after intensive inner preparation. Rudolf Steiner had given Ita Wegman an esoteric exercise that helped her to speak out of the "etheric,"[40] out of the sphere of life and resurrection, the world of the reappearance of the Christ.

Ita Wegman's unconditional faithfulness to the words originally spoken by Rudolf Steiner in the class lessons was no expression of inner conservatism but had to do with the essence of the lessons and her own way of relating to them. Rudolf Steiner used to open the gatherings with explanatory words about their meaning and mission (and the task of its members). The actual lessons that followed were "occult acts" during which the mantric verses were received by the members.[41] In some class lessons—and possibly also in conversations with Ita Wegman—Rudolf Steiner

Fig. 17: Ita Wegman

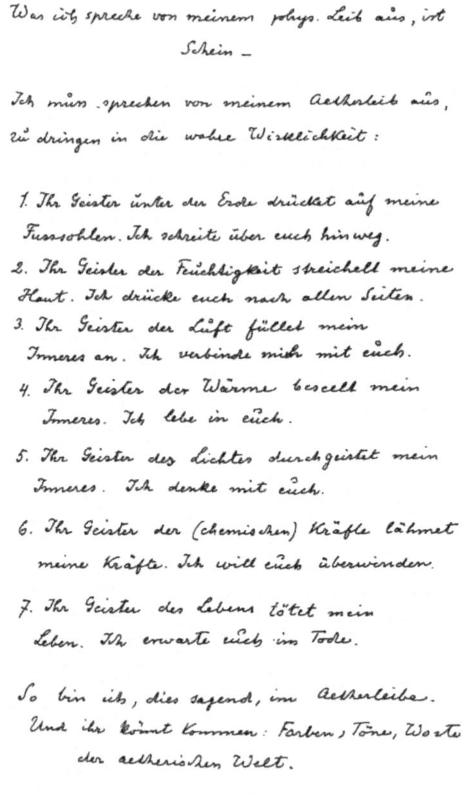

Was ich spreche von meinem phys. Leib aus, ist
Schein –

Ich muss sprechen von meinem Aetherleib aus,
zu dringen in die wahre Wirklichkeit:

1. Ihr Geister unter der Erde drücket auf meine
   Fusssohlen. Ich schreite über euch hinweg.
2. Ihr Geister der Feuchtigkeit streichelt meine
   Haut. Ich drücke euch nach allen Seiten.
3. Ihr Geister der Luft füllet mein
   Inneres an. Ich verbinde mich mit euch.
4. Ihr Geister der Wärme beseelt mein
   Inneres. Ich lebe in euch.
5. Ihr Geister des Lichtes durchgeistet mein
   Inneres. Ich denke mit euch.
6. Ihr Geister der (chemischen) Kräfte lähmet
   meine Kräfte. Ich will euch überwinden.
7. Ihr Geister des Lebens tötet mein
   Leben. Ich erwarte euch im Tode.

So bin ich, dies sagend, im Aetherleibe.
Und ihr könnt kommen: Farben, Töne, Worte
der aetherischen Welt.

Fig. 18: Handwritten notes for Ita Wegman from Rudolf Steiner

indicated that *all presentations* in the lessons, also the words spoken between the mantras, were powerful Michael revelations. ("*All the words spoken in this school are Michael words.*") Steiner referred to the mantras and to the (non-mantric) "content of what is presented here," pointing out that *both* these aspects of the esoteric lessons (that is, his own words also) could lose their "power" if they were passed on illegitimately.[42] In one of the "repeated lessons" of September 1924 he said:

> What is said here must therefore not be seen as my words. The lesson content must be seen as Michael's esoteric pronouncements in our time to those who feel they belong to him. What is contained in these lessons is Michael's message for our age. The content of these lessons will therefore be Michael's message for our age. It is from this that the anthroposophical movement will gain true spiritual strength.[43]

Rudolf Steiner pointed out that he was answerable to the spiritual powers that guided the anthroposophical movement for *each* single word spoken within the class lessons.[44] Ita Wegman would never have considered making changes to the lesson content and replacing any of Rudolf Steiner's words while claiming to deliver esoteric lessons of the Michael School. There is much to suggest that she would have seen such an attitude as impudence and as a serious misjudgment of the First Class. She would have been concerned that the First Class and the esoteric impulse could be weakened by it. ("*The content of these lessons will therefore be Michael's message for our age. It is from this that the anthroposophical movement will gain true spiritual strength.*" [Rudolf Steiner]) On June 22, 1924, Rudolf Steiner said in Dornach about the content of his Karma Lectures:

> We must be clear...that the contemplations cultivated here since the Christmas Conference must not be conveyed in any

other way by somebody else to this or that audience. The only possibility would be to read them out verbatim from a transcript if such a record was available.

These contents cannot be rephrased. I would object if that were to happen. Because it is important that with these serious and important matters every word and every sentence spoken here are carefully considered.⁴⁵

It was due to the Michael Mystery that Rudolf Steiner was able to give the Karma Lectures. Their content was conveyed *through* Rudolf Steiner whose individuality took responsibility for presenting this content in the "Christ language" of the dawning "age of light."⁴⁶ The same was true, at a higher level, for the esoteric lessons of the First Class.

◯

Ita Wegman thought even in the very first years after Rudolf Steiner's death that it was possible and appropriate to hold class meetings with a ritual beginning and end, where the mantras were read out with free observations weaving a bridge between them. Willem Zeylmans van Emmichoven, a member of the esoteric core of the Medical Section, did this in Holland.⁴⁷ But she felt that, as Rudolf Steiner's "helper" and closest coworker in the First Class, she was entitled and authorized to present Rudolf Steiner's own lesson in the language created by the initiated teacher, in order to bring back to life and resurrect in the souls of the class members his own "language body" (*"to bring what is written down back to life as it used to be"*). Until the end of her life Ita Wegman worked on this resurrection process, preparing it intensely and executing it in deepest devotion. At Christmas 1940, when she was in Ascona and unable to hold class lessons in Arlesheim, she wrote to her (disappointed) colleagues Marianne Fiechter-Bischof and Madeleine van Deventer:

I have the general impression that we should all be more active inwardly to make the Class more effective. There is something in me that expects thoughts of resurrection from all those who recently worked in the clinic, myself above all. All repetition at the same pace without dynamic enhancement tends to be paralyzing.[48]

The class must be resurrected and people must receive it in a new way.... I long to bring in something new, it lives in me, but it is so difficult if all one ever hears is that the class should be held in the old way. There must be a process of maturation so that the class can be raised to a higher level through us. This is what I am always working on.[49]

Ita Wegman expected greater "inner activity," even real "thoughts of resurrection," from the members of the School for Spiritual Science and from herself. She rejected people's preference for what had become tradition or habit and strove to raise the class to a higher level. She spoke of spiritual–social requirements that needed to be met within herself and in the community to enhance future lessons. Until the end Ita Wegman held class lessons in Casa Andrea Cristoforo and in Arlesheim, following on esoterically from Rudolf Steiner and working continuously with the structure, spiritual reality and living power of his words. She lived with the class contents, holding class lessons only when the social conditions were apposite. ("She would only agree once all discord between us had abated, which meant that sometimes we had to wait for a long time."[50]) On December 8, 1942, three months before her death, Ita Wegman held her last esoteric class in Arlesheim. In the way described by Marianne Fiechter-Bischof she read again the twelfth lesson.

The proximity of Rudolf Steiner's spiritual essence was tangible in her lessons. On behalf of the spiritual world Rudolf Steiner had imparted much in the lessons of *"what can be obtained in conversation with the Guardian of the threshold,*"[51] of what he himself had experienced in pursuing the path of Christian initiation in the age of Michael. In 1914, Rudolf Steiner had given the members of his Esoteric School the meditation cited below, saying: "If we meditate on the three formulae in the right way, with feeling, the higher hierarchies will promise to help us and we can say: "We draw closer to you!" And they will reach out to us and keep their promise." To Ita Wegman, his esoteric coworker in the School of Michael, his "dear friend and coworker in medicine and other fields of spiritual science, in all areas of spiritual research,"[52] Rudolf Steiner gave another meditation that promised her his help and support on her spiritual path:

> Ever shining, supreme light:
> To you I entrust my soul.—
> May the light of my soul weave
> with the weaving light of worlds.
> As light I feel,
> Light in the smallest point;
> Light that widens boundlessly;
> Light that carries my whole being
> To boundless spaces.
> Pure transparent light am I.
> I seize hold of the spirit world
> At the end of my soul of light,
> I hold the spirit world
> With my arms of light;
> I sense your presence,
> You want to carry me
> To worlds of light and spirit.[53]

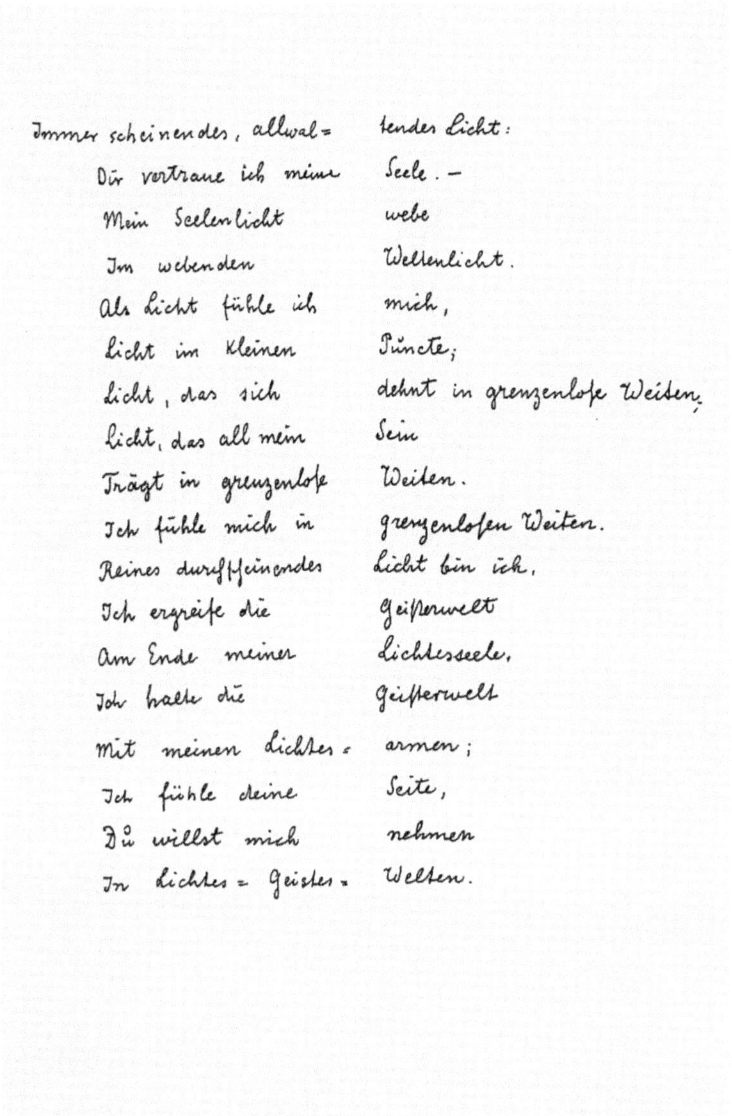

Immer scheinendes, allwal-
tendes Licht:
Dir vertraue ich meine
Seele. –
Mein Seelenlicht
webe
Im webenden
Wellenlicht.
Als Licht fühle ich
mich,
Licht im Kleinen
Puncte;
Licht, das sich
dehnt in grenzenlose Weiten,
Licht, das all mein
Sein
Trägt in grenzenlose
Weiten.
Ich fühle mich in
grenzenlosen Weiten.
Reines durchscheinendes
Licht bin ich.
Ich ergreife die
Geisterwelt
Am Ende meiner
Lichtesseele.
Ich halte die
Geisterwelt
Mit meinen Lichtes-
armen;
Ich fühle deine
Seite,
Du willst mich
nehmen
In Lichtes = Geister =
Welten.

Fig. 19: Rudolf Steiner: Handwritten verse for Ita Wegman

Chapter 6

Ita Wegman's Introductory Words to the Class Lessons

"And so I would appeal to your warmth of heart"
—Ita Wegman, (introducing the class lessons, 1925)

Meine lieben Freunde,
Bevor ich zur Klassenstunde übergeh
d. h. bevor ich dasjenige vorlese, was
Dr Steiner uns gegeben hat in der ersten Klassenstunde
~~die er~~ in Dornach am 15ten Februar 19 2.
~~gegeben~~ gehalten hat, möchte ich noch einiges
sagen.   nach der Weihnachtstagung
Dr Steiner gründete in der Hochschule für
Geisteswissenschaft eine esoterische Schule
die er die Michaël schule nannte und
die aus 3 Klassen bestehen sollte.
Die Michaëlschule ist also identisch mit
der Hochschule für Geisteswissenschaft,
Michaëlschule ist der esoterische Name
für die Hochschule für Geisteswissenschaft
Es wurde eben in Dornach mit dieser
Schule ein Anfang gemacht, und zwar
mit der ersten Klasse.
Leider musste es bei der 1sten Klasse
bleiben.
Dasjenige was vorgelesen wird, und es
kann nur vorgelesen werden, meine
lieben Freunde, weil dadurch Michaël
Worte unverändert, so wie Dr Steiner
sie gesprochen hat, Ihnen wiedergegeben
wird; dasjenige was vorgelesen wird

Ita Wegman's Introductory Words to the Class Lessons

My Dear Friends,

Before I begin the class lessons—that is, before I read what Dr. Steiner gave us in the first class lesson he held in Dornach on February 15, 1924—I would like to say a few words. After the Christmas Conference, Dr. Steiner founded along with the School for Spiritual Science an esoteric school that he called the Michael School, which was intended to consist of three classes. The Michael School is therefore identical with the School for Spiritual Science. "Michael School" is the esoteric name of the School for Spiritual Science. In Dornach, a beginning was made with this school—that is, with its first class. Sadly, there would be only a first class. What is being read—and it can only be read, my dear friends, because

sind also genaue Stenogramme von
Klassen Stunden, die unsere geliebter Lehrer in Dorna
gehalten hat.
Zum 1.sten Mal ist hier mit einem
Gesetz gebrochen: nämlich dass Esoterisches direct
aufgeschrieben wurde.
Es war niemals Sitte auch nicht in
früheren Zeiten, dass Esoterisches Weisheit
gut per Buchstabenschrift weiter gegeben
wurde. Immer war es durch mündliche
Überlieferung, dass Esoterisches bekannt
gegeben wurde.
Wir müssen uns dies wohl bewusst sein
Deshalb müssen wir mit viel Wärme, mit
viel Enthusiasmus an diese Klassenstunde
herantreten, um dasjenige, was nun da
Geschrieben steht wieder so lebendig zu
machen, als wie es gewesen war, als es
durch des grossen Meisters munde floss und
uns gegeben wurde.
Und so möchte ich appellieren an Ihre
Herzenswärme an Ihren vollen Enthusiasmus
diese Stunde in der richtigen Art und
Gesinnung mit zu machen, und zu erleben.

Ita Wegman's Introductory Words to the Class Lessons

in this way Michael's words are repeated to you unaltered as Dr. Steiner spoke them—what is being read are exact transcriptions of class lessons that our beloved teacher held at Dornach. A law was broken here for the first time when esoteric contents were written down. It never happened, not even in ancient times, that esoteric contents were written down. Esoteric knowledge was passed on only orally. We must be well aware of this and approach the class lessons with great warmth and with enthusiasm to bring back to life what is written down here, as it was when it flowed to us from the lips of the great Master. I appeal to your warmth of heart, to your full enthusiasm, that you approach this lesson in the right way and experience it with the right inner attitude.

Meine lieben Freunde

Nachdem bei Ihnen die Klassenstunden durch Graf Polzer in so schöner Weise übermittelt worden sind und auch in der gleicher Art fortgesetzt werden können, habe ich gedacht, anstatt weiter zu gehen nun mal eine Klassenstunde zu wiederholen und so werde ich anfangen Ihnen diejenige Klassenstunde vorzulesen, die Dr. Steiner am 14ten März 1924 in Dornach gehalten hat. Es handelt sich in dieser Klassenstunde um weitere Belehrungen vom Hüter der Schwelle, nachdem die Erlebnisse mit den Tieren uns erklärt worden sind.

Das was ich also vorbringe, sind Michaelsworte unverändert so wie Dr. Steiner sie ausgesprochen hat.

Sie sind aufgeschrieben worden, und so ist zum 1sten Mal hier mit einem Gesetz gebrochen, nämlich dass Esoterisches direkt aufgeschrieben wurde. Es war niemals Sitte auch nicht in früheren Zeiten, dass Esoterische Weisheit gut per Buch statuendlich weiter gegeben wurde. Immer war es durch mündliche Überlieferung dass Esoterisches weiter gegeben wurde. Wir müssen uns dies wohl bewusst sein

Ita Wegman's Introductory Words to the Class Lessons

My Dear Friends,

The class lessons have been beautifully conveyed to you by Count Polzer and can continue in the same manner. I therefore thought that, instead of moving on, I would repeat a class lesson. Therefore, I will begin to read to you the class lesson that Dr. Steiner held on March 14, 1924, in Dornach. This class lesson is about further instructions from the Guardian of the Threshold, after the experiences with the beasts have been explained to us. What I present are Michael words unaltered and as Dr. Steiner spoke them. They were written down, and so for the first time a law was broken. It never happened, not in ancient times either, that esoteric contents were written down. Esoteric knowledge was always passed on only orally. We must be well aware of this. When our beloved

1)
Als unser ~~unvergessliche~~ geliebte ~~Meister und teuerer Führer~~ Lehrer Rudolf Steiner uns auf dem phys Plan verließ, war eine der wichtigsten Fragen, ~~die den Vorstand beschäftigte,~~ wie die Fortführung der Esoterik zu gestalten sei.
Diese Esoterik war auf dem Vordergrund des Anthroposophischen Wirkens gestellt worden.
Es war uns bewusst, dass es sich bei dieser Fortführung der Esoterik nicht darum handeln könnte, neues in der Esoterik zu geben.
Die Fortführung musste in dem Sinne aufgefasst werden, dass das gegebene Weisheitsgut in der richtigen Art gehütet werde. Dass die Wiederholung der schon gegebenen Klassenstunden in der richtigen Art geschieht.
Diese Esoterik, dieses Weisheitsgut ist der Inhalt der Michaelschule und wurde in der ersten Klasse der Hochschule gegeben.
Als Rudolf Steiner diese Michaelschule einsetzte, eine, von der geistigen Welt gestiftete Institution, wie er sagte, wurde ich von ihm als seine Mitarbeiterin

teacher Rudolf Steiner left us on the physical plane, one of the most important questions was how the esoteric lessons were to continue. This esotericism has been a priority in the anthroposophic activities. We knew that the continuation of the esotericism did not imply the presentation of new esoteric results. Continuation had to mean that the given wisdom was guarded in the right way. That repetition of the given class lessons takes place in the right way. This esotericism, this gift of wisdom, is the content of the Michael School and was given in the First Class of the School for Spiritual Science. When Rudolf Steiner instituted this Michael School as an establishment founded from the spiritual world, as he said, I was named by him as his assistant in this school. Therefore, my dear friends, I felt, after the demise of our teacher, not released from my commitment toward the Michael School; on the contrary,

2/

in dieser Schule bezeichnet.
Deshalb meine lieben Freunde, fühlte ich mich, nach dem Tode unseres Lehrers nicht gelöst von den Verpflichtungen der Michaelschule gegenüber, in Gegenteil ich fühlte mich noch mehr dann je mit ihr verbunden. Die Michaelschule als Institution der geistigen Welt, die Worte Dr. Steiners musste ich ernst nehmen, da ich die Geistige Welt und die aus ihr herausströmenden Gesetzmäsigkeiten als Realitäten ansehe.

Aus dieser Situation heraus obliegt mir mit Einverständnis der andern Vorstandsmitglieder die Pflicht das was durch Rudolf Steiner an die Mitglieder der 1ten Klasse der Hochschule für Geisteswissenschaft mitgeteilt wurde zu hüten und zu wiederholen. Ich werde Ihnen jetzt die Worte, die Dr. Steiner zur Einleitung schon konnten Klassenstunden gegeben für neue Ungeheilte werden in der das Wort Dr. Steiners offiziell wiedergegeben wurde in Paris, in Bern, zu späteren Folge in Wien Hamburg vorlesen.

So möchte ich liebe Freunde vor Ihnen stehen und das Wort Rudolf Steiner Ihnen wieder geben, seine Liebe und seine Treue zu Ihnen weiter fortsetzen, so weit es in meiner Ri

Ita Wegman's Introductory Words to the Class Lessons

I felt bound to it more than ever. The Michael School as an institution of the spiritual world, the words of Dr. Steiner, I had to take seriously, since I see the spiritual world and the laws that stream down from it as realities. Out of this situation arises the task for me, with the agreement of the other members of the Executive Council in Dornach, to guard and repeat what was imparted by Dr. Steiner to the members of the First Class of the School for Spiritual Science in Dornach. Class lessons that faithfully repeated Dr. Steiner's words could already be held in Paris, in Dornach, in Vienna, Hamburg. Therefore, I would like to stand before you, dear friends, and repeat Rudolf Steiner's words, carry forward his love and loyalty to you to the best of my ability. I will now read to you the words that Dr. Steiner used to speak as an introduction for members who had newly joined.[1]

Appendix

The Relationship of Teachers, Physicians, and Priests to the School for Spiritual Science in 1924

In their first faculty meeting with Rudolf Steiner following the Christmas Conference, the teachers of the Stuttgart Waldorf School asked him how, in the future, the school ought to relate to the Goetheanum and the School for Spiritual Science. At the meeting that took place in Stuttgart on February 5, 1924, ten days before the first Class Lesson, Rudolf Steiner stated clearly that he did not favor the direct affiliation of the "Independent Waldorf School" to the School for Spiritual Science in Dornach, particularly also with the public in mind. He did, however, support the idea that the "faculty of teachers as a whole" or *"those within the faculty who wish to do so, [should] join...the School for Spiritual Science, not as private individuals but as teachers of the school."*[1]

There is no doubt that Rudolf Steiner found a "living relationship" between the teaching faculty and the School for Spiritual Science desirable and necessary since it would carry the Dornach impulse into the life of the Waldorf school. "The—so far mostly theoretical—connection with anthroposophical pedagogy would be filled with life and, as a result, the faculty as a whole, or the individuals in it, would be inspired by the impulses accessible to teachers who are members of the School for Spiritual Science."[2]

When this discussion took place—five weeks after the Christmas Conference—most of the Stuttgart teachers had written to Rudolf Steiner in Dornach to apply for admission to the First Class. Rudolf Steiner nevertheless pointed out at that faculty meeting how meaningful and essential membership in the Dornach School for Spiritual Science was for *all* teachers. Not only would it give "inspiration and insight to their individual lives," it would allow them to contribute actively to the success of the School for Spiritual Science as an academic institution that strove to find answers to questions in the sciences and arts.[3] Rudolf Steiner underlined the importance of teachers not only joining as individuals on their path of inner development. His exact words were: "Are the teachers of the school content to belong to the School for Spiritual Science in Dornach as private individuals, or do they want to join as a faculty so that each of them joins 'as a teacher of the Independent Waldorf School?' If the faculty joins, the teachers force the Pedagogical Section in Dornach to concern itself with the Independent Waldorf School instead of focusing on questions of education in general. There is a big difference between the two."[4] It was obvious which of the two options Rudolf Steiner favored (and had to favor for spiritual reasons).

When shortly afterwards Lilly Kolisko asked Rudolf Steiner's permission to take down his Dornach class lessons in shorthand so that she could present them to the Stuttgart anthroposophists, he consented, pointing out that she should hold the lessons not to the anthroposophical group there but to the *faculty of teachers* at the Waldorf school because they were a group he was able and willing to work with esoterically. ("Dr. Steiner continued: 'Would you not want to impart the lessons to the teachers of the Waldorf school?' Of course I was only too happy to do that and

Dr. Steiner promised to issue the necessary membership cards *for the entire faculty*."⁵

We can assume that the Stuttgart teachers decided to follow the direction Rudolf Steiner had outlined and recommended to them on February 5, 1924. It was the logical and right step to take. The Dornach School for Spiritual Science wanted, and needed, to be active and productive in the various fields, including education. Affiliation to Dornach was not only a matter of personal inner development, which was implied anyway in being a member of the Anthroposophical Society or a Waldorf teacher. The impulses of the Christmas Conference had to come to life in the Stuttgart school. The faculty of teachers could be an esoteric organ. ("The faculty must form a center from which something can radiate out."⁶) It was with this in mind that Lilly Kolisko held class lessons for the community of teachers.

The public teachers' conference with the title "Education in Today's Personal and Cultural Life," which was held at the Stuttgart Waldorf School between April 7 and 13, 1924, was the first event of its kind to be organized and carried jointly by the Executive Council of the Anthroposophical Society and the Faculty of Teachers of the Waldorf school.⁷ Rudolf Steiner himself devised the program and submitted it to his colleagues of the "Esoteric Council" in Dornach ("to be circulated for written consent"). He was the first to sign it, followed by Albert Steffen, Ita Wegman, Marie Steiner, Günther Wachsmuth, and Elisabeth Vreede.⁸ A new era of cooperation with the School for Spiritual Science in Dornach began for the faculty of the Waldorf school.

The situation of the physicians needs to be looked at in a more differentiated way since they did not form a community or homogeneous group. They worked each in their own context—a hospital or private practice—with their own particular tasks, conditions and goals. Many of them probably decided personally for themselves to establish a "connection with Dornach."

For the researcher who seeks to understand the situation that evolved after the Christmas Conference, the activities surrounding a group of medical students and young doctors are of particular interest. This initially rather informal association of "young medics" who were dissatisfied with the conservatism of the anthroposophical physicians first approached Rudolf Steiner in the fall of 1922. Enthused by a spirit of departure, they sought for ways of making medicine "truly humane."[9] In January and April 1924, Rudolf Steiner gave courses especially for that group: they were in fact the first academic courses to take place after the Christmas Conference; esoteric courses with a mantric structure that brought the spirit of the class lessons to a specialist professional field.[10] Most of the "young medics" were very young and not all were members of the Anthroposophical Society, nor did they necessarily consider applying for membership in the School for Spiritual Science in Dornach. But Rudolf Steiner decided to admit the group as a whole before the Easter Course was due to begin. Madeleine van Deventer wrote: "It seems important that immediately after arriving in Dornach we received our certificates as members of the First Class of the School for Spiritual Science, even those who had not applied yet."[11]

In the class lesson of Good Friday, April 18, 1924, Rudolf Steiner evidently referred to his newsletter to the young doctors of March 11 as a letter to class members *regarding the work of the School for Spiritual Science*, although he had not admitted the group yet at the time of writing. (That only happened immediately before the class lesson.) These newsletters were to be a means of informing members of the School for Spiritual Science about the work that was being done in the various specialist fields[12] and about "what streams through this School in Dornach."[13]

Rudolf Steiner began this process of communication with the medical newsletter he wrote on March 11, 1924, using it to answer questions sent in by participants of the January course. The answers were signed by him and Ita Wegman. The newsletter opens with the words: "We promised at the Christmas Conference to keep you informed about the direction of the Medical Section at the Goetheanum. In fulfillment of that promise we now send this first newsletter to all those who are united with us in the desire to nurture the medical work. It is carried by the spirit that brought us together during the medical courses in the New Year."[14] Rudolf Steiner and Ita Wegman referred to an existing connection—an esoteric connection that had been created by the course—with the School for Spiritual Science and its Medical Section ("to those who are *united with us* in the desire to nurture the medical work.")

The courses of January and April 1924 constituted the first esoteric and exoteric teaching offered by the Medical Section at the Goetheanum. At the same time they were the first building blocks for that section as the medical faculty of the new School for Spiritual Science. The course members were not only expected to listen to the lectures and absorb their content. They were called upon to become active as a community that was inspired by the Dornach impulse. Rudolf Steiner spoke of the group as "affiliated to Dornach" and of a connection "among you and with us here." About the general situation and the new beginning of the anthroposophical movement after the Christmas Conference he said: "From this moment onward we must see a change in the anthroposophical movement, also in the various fields of practical application. The esoteric path must not be a sideline. Your whole life must be permeated by the esoteric impulses."[15]

The Medical Section of the School for Spiritual Science was clearly designated as a center of research and teaching and it was therefore essential and logical for the young doctors and medical students to remain connected with Dornach. Rudolf Steiner saw his own initiated work within all the sections as part of the Esoteric School and he expected the same of the professional groups that had taken on responsibility for the School. Rudolf Steiner's specialist research and his collaboration, as an initiate, with the section leaders formed the center of each section's spiritual research and teaching. From this center spiritual-scientific support would flow to the various specialist fields: initiation knowledge, research methods and assignments that would benefit members of the School for Spiritual Science in their own field of expertise, and through them the world at large. "We want to remain united, my dear friends, so that you will continue to have your center here in Dornach at the Goetheanum and that *this center can, through you, work into the world.*"[16]

The Course for Young Doctors, as an esoteric medical community, became the "esoteric center of the Medical Section." It was with this core group that Rudolf Steiner intended to institute a new medical mystery school and build up the Medical Section. His premature death prevented him from realizing these intentions.[17]

∽

Gottfried Husemann wrote in an essay about the relationship of the Christian Community priests with the School for Spiritual Science in Dornach and the last course on the Apocalypse that Rudolf Steiner gave in September 1924 in Dornach: "'I will admit you all to the First Class of the School for Spiritual Science', he [Rudolf Steiner] said right at the beginning. And that is what he did in the next few days. As a result the priests were able to take part, not only in the lectures on the Apocalypse and the evening lectures [on Karmic Relations], but also in the first course of the Michael School. 'You will also receive the letters of the School for Spiritual Science,' he added. He was sadly no longer able to write those letters. 'Relations with the anthroposophical movement will grow ever more intimate.'"[18]

Like the teachers of the Stuttgart school, some Christian Community priests had, in February 1924, consulted Rudolf Steiner individually on how the Christian Community was to relate in future with the General Anthroposophical Society and its newly founded School for Spiritual Science in Dornach. By then, he had agreed to more intensive collaboration and to the admission to the First Class and had mentioned his intention to send out regular newsletters about the work of the School for Spiritual Science in the future.

Rudolf Steiner had no plans of introducing a Theological Section in Dornach. Instead he asked for the research, teaching and ritual practice performed at the Christian Community in Stuttgart since its inception in the fall of 1922 to be continued. He was nonetheless emphatically in favor of the priests' active involvement, as individuals and as an esoteric community, in the work that had begun in Dornach. Following a request by Friedrich Rittelmeyer, Rudolf Steiner proceeded to accept, in September 1924, priests into the School for Spiritual Science who had not been members of the Anthroposophical Society for two years yet or who were not members at all, just as he done with the young physicians and medical students half a year earlier.

There is no doubt that the Christian Community and the personalities who mainly carried it were important for Rudolf Steiner. In a faculty meeting at the Stuttgart Waldorf school he said in June 1924: "You must not forget that the priests of the Christian Community are anthroposophists too. And they have made considerable progress in their inner development in a very short time. They have advanced in their soul life in an exemplary way in the short period that the Christian Community has existed. This might not apply to each single individual, but it is generally true. They have been a great blessing in all areas."[19] In the course on the Apocalypse Rudolf Steiner even spoke of "what can make the Christian Community an essential pillar of the new mysteries."[20] In doing so he indirectly included the Christian Community in the School for Spiritual Science in Dornach. Elsewhere he said about the School for Spiritual Science: "The mysteries receded when the time had come for humanity to develop freedom. Now it is time to find the mysteries again. We must know that we need to actively try to find the mysteries again today. This is why the Christmas Conference was held. It is urgently necessary that there is a place on Earth where mysteries can be founded again. The Anthroposophical Society must become the path that will lead to the renewal of the mysteries."[21]

෴

There are many historical questions that have not yet been researched or illuminated sufficiently. The transformation (or transformability) of the School for Spiritual Science of 1924/1925, which was a real center of initiation owing to Rudolf Steiner's presence, now remains—*without* him—a central task and problem. But historical investigation reveals how important inner affiliation to the School for Spiritual Science was for Rudolf Steiner—not just for individuals, but also for esoteric groups. The esoteric communities are in their professional orientation inseparably linked with what flows to civilization from the School for Spiritual Science in Dornach. What "the world and civilization need today from the Goetheanum for their further development"[22] could be brought into the world only by spiritual associations, by people who stood behind Dornach and its spiritual orientation and who were prepared to apply this spirituality consistently and courageously in practice in the various fields. "I am here to represent the Anthroposophy that emanates from the Goetheanum."[23]

Notes

References to the works of Rudolf Steiner given in the following notes refer to the pages of the German editions unless otherwise stated. The quotations in the main text and notes have mostly been newly translated; those taken from existing translations were, in some places, adjusted to give consistency of style and terminology.

Preface

1. Ludwig Polzer-Hoditz: "Personal communication" of Dec. 1, 1935. From Johannes Kiersch: *A History of the School for Spiritual Science: The First Class*. London: Temple Lodge, 2006, p. 234.

2. Cf. Rudolf Steiner's essays and lectures on the theme in: *Die Konstitution der Allgemeinen Anthroposophischen Gesellschaft und der Freien Hochschule für Geisteswissenschaft*. Dornach 1987, especially the passage quoted in note 140 below. (English: *The Christmas Conference: For the Foundation of the General Anthroposophical Society, 1923/1924* [The Collected Works of Rudolf Steiner (CW) 260a]. Hudson, NY: Anthroposophic Press, 1990).

3. Rudolf Steiner addressed this in several class lessons, beginning in the fourth which took place Mar. 7, 1924. There he reported that a member was excluded from the school three weeks after its inauguration. Even at the end of the nineteenth class lesson on August 2, 1924, that concluded the cycle of First Class instructions, Rudolf Steiner found it necessary to return to its serious problems: "Some people who applied and were admitted to the Esoteric School have a peculiar way of observing its rules. I had to speak of that yesterday already. It is difficult to believe, but some members hold the blue esoteric cards and occupy their seats here. Yet it happened three times that notebooks—in fact it was one case and two notebooks—with the School's mantric verses were left behind. The case with the machine-typed verses was found outside in the street. One

notebook was copied from as I described yesterday. The other one was left in the Glass House. As a consequence we had to exclude three members before this class lesson which brings the number of exclusions to nineteen. I would expect those who hear about the significance of this school here to take it more seriously. One member loses the verses in the street, another leaves them behind in the Glass House and we are forced to exclude three prominent members. I assure you, my dear sisters and brothers: everything that was said in the beginning, and repeatedly since then, about the need to observe strictly the school's regulations must be observed as strictly. A serious esoteric school like ours is only sustainable if its members observe what is asked of them by the spiritual powers guiding it. That is the way of the truly occult. The things that have been going on in the Anthroposophical Society must stop. It is important that a matter of so serious a nature is approached with the greatest seriousness." (Rudolf Steiner: *Esoterische Unterweisungen für die erste Klasse der Freien Hochschule für Geisteswissenschaft am Goetheanum*. CW 270b. Dornach 1992, p. 176 ["Esoteric Instructions for the First Class of the University for Spiritual Science at the Goetheanum," 4 vols.; unavailable in English]) In 1992, all of Rudolf Steiner's class lessons were published (on the basis of a former three-volume manuscript dating from 1977). The decision to publish them was justified in an article titled "Vorbemerkungen zur Veröffentlichung der Inhalte der ersten Klasse der Freien Hochschule für Geisteswissenschaft." These considerations regarding the publication of the class lessons was signed on behalf of the *Rudolf Steiner Estate Administration* by Edwin Froböse, Hella Wiesberger and Gian-Andrea Balastère and on behalf of the School for Spiritual Science by Manfred Schmidt-Brabant, Hagen Biesantz and Jörgen Smit. The article is part of volume 1 of CW 270a, pp. ix–xv.

4   Cf. *Denkschrift über Angelegenheiten der Anthroposophischen Gesellschaft in den Jahren 1925 bis 1935*. Dornach 1935; Emanuel Zeylmans van Emmichoven: *Who was Ita Wegman? A Documentation*. vol. 3. Spring Valley 1995; Johannes Kiersch: *A History of the School for Spiritual Science: The First Class*.

5   Albert Steffen: Introduction to the first Class Lesson held by Dr. Wegman in Dornach on June 4, 1925. Quoted from Johannes Kiersch: *A History of the School for Spiritual Science: The First Class*. p. 177. ("It is incumbent on me, the second chair, to reflect on the solemn warning that the School of Michael is the heart of the Society, the heart of the Anthroposophical Society. With the

class lessons, Rudolf Steiner has given us something that is most sacred. May all hold it sacred..." Ibid.)

6   Cf. in particular Johannes Kiersch's judicious description in: *A History of the School for Spiritual Science: The First Class*, pp. 41–66.

7   Rudolf Steiner: *Esoterische Unterweisungen für die erste Klasse der Freien Hochschule für Geisteswissenschaft am Goetheanum 1924*. CW 270c, pp. 126f.

8   Kurt Franz David published such a history of the First Class in 1974 for the Executive Council in Dornach. ("Die Einrichtung der Ersten Klasse durch Rudolf Steiner und deren Schicksale bis zur Gegenwart." Hectographed manuscript, Goetheanum Archives.)

9   Johannes Kiersch: *A History of the School for Spiritual Science: The First Class*, p. 67.

10 Ibid., p. 59.

11 Ibid., p. 64.

12 Ibid., p. xiii and 59.

13 Marie Steiner, quoted from Johannes Kiersch, ibid.

14 "Out of what you have heard, out of the mantras, you can develop a form of work with people who want to do it with you." (Rudolf Steiner to Ludwig Count Polzer-Hoditz, quoted from Johannes Kiersch, p. 117.)

15 Marie Steiner wrote in one of her notebooks that Rudolf Steiner gave the following "guidelines" for groups of individuals "intent on working through and living the mantric class verses together": "Speakers of the mantras should work out for themselves what to say to connect the verses. He [Rudolf Steiner] encouraged independent work with the verses as long as it was based on the wisdom he had conveyed. But, above all, it was important to experience the verses." (Notebook 20. First published in the editor's preface to: Rudolf Steiner, *Esoterische Unterweisungen für die erste Klasse der Freien Hochschule für Geisteswissenschaft am Goetheanum 1924*. CW 270a, p. xiii.)

16 In a letter from Aberdeen dated June 11, 1942, Maria Röschl reminded Ita Wegman of a conversation between them just before she left for Costa Rica: "We were walking in the garden in front of your clinic when you told me so warmly that, wherever I was, I ought to work with people on the First Class, should the necessity arise." (Ita Wegman Archives)

17 "The [class] lessons [in Dornach] left a deep impression on me and I asked myself: What about all the members who don't live in Dornach and are unable to hear Dr. Steiner's wonderful communications? Was there a way of making the content of these lessons

available to other members? I asked Dr. Wegman, the society secretary. 'How would you envisage that?' she asked and I suggested giving an account of the lessons to a small group in Stuttgart, the 'Group of Thirty' for instance. Dr. Wegman promised to ask Dr. Steiner who then asked me to come and see him. I will try to repeat our conversation as truly as possible. Dr. Steiner said: 'Dr. Wegman spoke to me of your intention to convey the class lessons to a group of members. I like the idea. But why the 'Group of Thirty'? They are not a group I can work with esoterically.' I replied that I had only used that group as an example when I expressed my wish to convey the class content to a smaller group of people. Dr. Steiner continued: 'Would you not want to impart the lessons to the teachers of the Waldorf school?' Of course I was only too happy to do that and Dr. Steiner promised to issue the necessary membership cards for the entire faculty.... I felt I was not capable of presenting the lessons and asked Dr. Steiner's permission to write them down. He gave it though nobody else was allowed to copy down the lessons." (Lilly Kolisko: *Eugen Kolisko. Ein Lebensbild*. Gerabronn/Crailsheim 1961, pp. 90f.; cf. Johannes Kiersch: *A History of the School for Spiritual Science: The First Class*. p. 70.) Johannes Kiersch explains the situation at the Stuttgart School: "A few days before the lessons started, the faculty of the Waldorf school had a lengthy meeting with Rudolf Steiner. It was the first visit since the Christmas Conference and they asked for clarification as to how the Waldorf school related to the newly founded School for Spiritual Science, with almost all of them asking to be admitted to the First Class" (Ibid., p. 71). Once all nineteen lessons had been given, Lilly Kolisko described her experiences with the teachers and the class lessons in a letter to Ita Wegman on November 2, 1924: "Looking at the faculty of teachers before and after Christmas [before and after the Christmas Conference, that is, before and after the institution of the First Class] shows that many things have changed. The class lessons have brought the whole faculty closely together. The faculty has really become something recently. I would say that a certain gravity is noticeable, a sacred gravity as such a holy cause requires. 'The faculty must form a center,' as the doctor had once said to me, 'from which something can radiate out.' I believe that this center is growing ever stronger.... I must also tell you how remarkably my relationship with the teachers has changed since I am allowed to read the lessons. Not a night passes when I do not dream of one of them. Even people I hardly know appear. When I was in Holland, I dreamed the entire faculty meeting, for instance in the night from Tuesday to Wednesday. The meeting takes place on Tuesday evenings and it was confirmed to me that my dream was a true reflection of the entire faculty meeting" (Ita Wegman Archives).

18   On March 15, 1925, only two weeks before his death, Rudolf Steiner wrote to the faculty of teachers in Stuttgart: "My dear teachers of the Waldorf school, I feel greatly deprived because I cannot come to see you. I must place the important task of making decisions that I used to share with you since the school's foundation into your hands entirely. It is a time of trial. I am with you in thought and I cannot do more without taking the risk of extending the time of physical illness indefinitely. *May active power of thought unite us,/ Since parted in space we needs must be./ May what has been achieved so far,/ strongly work among the teachers of this school./ May it live within their counseling,/ since the counselor, who would so gladly come,/ has wings no longer free to fly.* Let us strive even more intensely for spiritual communion as long as we cannot do more. The Waldorf school is truly a child in need of care, but it is, above all, living proof of how fruitful Anthroposophy is within human spiritual life. If all teachers in their hearts remain aware of this fruitfulness, the good spirits that watch over this school can be active and the work of the teachers will be imbued by divine spiritual power. With this in mind I send you my warmest regards and greetings. I enclose a short letter to the pupils which I ask you to read out to the classes. With warmest regards, Rudolf Steiner" (in: Rudolf Steiner: *Die Konstitution der Allgemeinen Anthroposophischen Gesellschaft und der Freien Hochschule für Geisteswissenschaft.* pp. 404f. [English trans.: *The Foundation Stone/The Life, Nature & Cultivation of Anthroposophy* (CW 260a). London: Rudolf Steiner Press, 1996]. English translation of verse from *Towards the Deepening of Waldorf Education. Excerpts from the work of Rudolf Steiner. Essays and Documents.* Published by the Pedagogical Section of the School for Spiritual Science. Goetheanum. Dornach, p. 83. Tr. R. Everett).

19   There is plenty of evidence to suggest that, after Steiner's death, Ita Wegman saw the reading of class lessons as her *very own* task. Faced with the looming crisis in Dornach—and maybe because Rudolf Steiner had, in the sixteenth lesson, referred to the "esoteric council" as the leadership of the School—she later proposed that all council members, and they alone, should take on the reading of class lessons (which excluded Lilly Kolisko). Wegman's "postulation" of restricting the reading privilege to members of the

Dornach council has provoked criticism from historiographers, Johannes Kiersch included. But her request is no disconcerting call for hierarchy and exclusivity (based on a centralistic leadership model), although it might seem so at first glance. Closer investigation reveals that Ita Wegman was mostly driven by the wish to respect Rudolf Steiner's esoteric work and the spirit of the Christmas Conference. Probably not even Ita Wegman understood Rudolf Steiner's attitude with regard to Lilly Kolisko. It is unlikely that Steiner allowed Lilly Kolisko—and her alone—to read out the transcript of the class lessons because she was the first to ask, as Johannes Kiersch suggests. ("A possible reason may be that Lilly Kolisko was the first ever to ask for it, doing so in February 1924, for the specific purpose of passing the mantras on to people she knew in Stuttgart. He was following the principle of developing the School 'from below,' according to members' needs, and therefore gave a loving response to Lilly Kolisko's request." *A History of the School for Spiritual Science: The First Class*, p. 74. It is important not to overlook Lilly Kolisko's spiritual essence, her deep morality, selflessness, conscientiousness and loyalty and her close cooperation with Rudolf Steiner on a Christ-permeated approach to the sciences. Rudolf Steiner allowed Lilly Kolisko to speak at length at the Christmas Conference (on the day he recited the rhythm: "*Light Divine, / Sun of Christ / The Elemental Spirits / In the East, West, North, South hear this. / May human beings hear it*"). When they first met in Vienna in 1915 he said to her: "You can see the ether" (cf. Peter Selg: *Anfänge anthroposophischer Heilkunst*. Dornach 2000, pp. 133f.) . Not only did Rudolf Steiner give permission to Lilly Kolisko, who was not a physician, to attend his lectures to young physicians and medical students, he allowed her to take the lectures down in shorthand and read them out in Stuttgart (Cf. Peter Selg: *Die Briefkorrespondenz der 'jungen Mediziner'. Eine dokumentarische Studie zur Rezeption von Rudolf Steiner's 'Jungmediziner'-Kursen*. Dornach 2005, pp. 35ff). There is evidence to suggest that Rudolf Steiner would have liked Lilly Kolisko to lead the Science Section in Dornach as this would have enabled him to continue working with her (within the esoteric community of sections). But this was not possible, partly because she could not leave Stuttgart. ("The section leaders must live here in Dornach." Rudolf Steiner: *Die Weihnachtstagung zur Begründung der Allgemeinen Anthroposophischen Gesellschaft 1923/24*. CW 260. Dornach 1995, pp. 113f.)

Notes

20 Lecture given in Dornach on Apr. 14, 1935. Cited from Emanuel Zeylmans van Emmichoven: *Wer war Ita Wegman. Eine Dokumentation*, vol. 3, p. 335.
21 Emanuel Zeylmans van Emmichoven: *Who was Ita Wegman? A Documentation*, 3 vols. Spring Valley, NY, 1995. Tr. D. Winter.
22 Johannes Kiersch: *A History of the School for Spiritual Science: The First Class*, p. 139.
23 Ibid., p. 59.
24 Ibid., pp. 144f.
25 Cf. main text, pp. 92f. [chap. 5].
26 Liane Collot d'Herbois: "A Lighter Aspect of the Personality of Ita Wegman." In: *Hefte des Ita Wegman Fonds für soziale und therapeutische Hilfstätigkeiten*. Michaelmas 1989, p. 17. Cf. also Peter Selg: *Liane Collot d'Herbois und Ita Wegman*. Dornach 2008, pp. 9ff.
27 Ita Wegman: *An die Freunde*. Arlesheim 1986, p. 11.
28 Rudolf Steiner: *Esoterische Unterweisungen für die Erste Klasse der Freien Hochschule für Geisteswissenschaft am Goetheanum 1924*. CW 270b, p. 90.
29 Rudolf Steiner to Ludwig Count Polzer-Hoditz. Dornach, November 11, 1924. Cited from Johannes Kiersch: *A History of the School for Spiritual Science: The First Class*. p. 117.
30 Ita Wegman: Letter to Maria Röschl of February 22, 1935. Ita Wegman Archives.
31 Ita Wegman: Notes for a lecture at Casa Andrea Cristoforo on March 30, 1941. Ita Wegman Archives.
32 Michael Bauer: "Über die Schülerschaft" (1925). In: *Gesammelte Werke*, vol. 2. Ed. Christoph Rau. Stuttgart 1987, p. 315.
33 On the mystery background and aspects of Rudolf Steiner's collaboration with Ita Wegman, cf. vols. 1 and 2 of Emanuel Zeylmans van Emmichoven's fundamental study: *Who was Ita Wegman? A Documentation*, vols. 1, 2, and 3. I do not repeat Zeylman's conclusions in my work but build on them. For Zeylman's further work, see note 176.
34 Ita Wegman: Letter to Ludwig Count Polzer-Hoditz, July 9, 1935 (Ita Wegman Institute).

Chapter 1

1 Rudolf Steiner: *Esoterische Unterweisungen für die erste Klasse der Freien Hochschule für Geisteswissenschaft am Goetheanum 1924*. CW 270b, p. 31.

2   Rudolf Steiner: *Die Konstitution der Allgmeinen Anthroposophischen Gesellschaft und der Freien Hochschule für Geisteswissenschaft.* CW 260a, p. 100.
3   Rudolf Steiner: *Esoterische Unterweisungen für die erste Klasse der Freien Hochschule für Geisteswissenschaft am Goetheanum 1924.* CW 270b, p. 90.
4   Rudolf Steiner: *Esoterische Unterweisungen für die erste Klasse der Freien Hochschule für Geisteswissenschaft am Goetheanum 1924.* CW 270a, p. 1 ("Freedom, Immortality, Social Life"; not available in English).
5   Ibid.
6   The name of the building (that referred to "Johannes Thomasius, the central character in Rudolf Steiner's mystery plays) was changed to "Goetheanum" at the general meeting of the "Johannesbau-Verein" [Johannes Building Association] of Oct. 21, 1917, at the request of Mieta Wallers. The meeting was preceded by lectures in Basel where Rudolf Steiner said: "I would prefer to call this...anthroposophical view of the world, that arises from scientific research in the way I indicated, after the sources from which it arises for me (if it was not for the danger of being misunderstood I would always call it that). I would like to call this philosophy "Goetheanism," and I would like to call the building in Dornach, that is dedicated to it, the "Goetheanum," if that would not provoke a series of misunderstandings" (*Freiheit, Unsterblichkeit, Soziales Leben.* CW 72. Dornach 1990, p. 50).
7   Rudolf Steiner: *Der Goetheanumgedanke inmitten der Kulturkrisis der Gegenwart.* CW 36. Dornach 1961, p. 309. ("The Goetheanum Idea in the Middle of the Present Cultural Crisis: Collected Essays from the Periodical Das Goetheanum 1921–1925"; not available in English).
8   Rudolf Steiner: *Inneres Wesen und Leben zwischen Tod und neuer Geburt.* CW 153. Dornach 1997, pp. 14f. (emphasis added). English trans.: *The Inner Nature of Man: And Our Life between Death and Rebirth.* London: Rudolf Steiner Press, 1994).
9   Friedrich Rittelmeyer: *Meine Lebensbegegnung mit Rudolf Steiner.* Stuttgart 1983, p. 128.
10 Cf. Rudolf Steiner: *Geisteswissenschaft und Medizin.* (English trans.: *Introducing Anthroposophical Medicine* [CW 312]. Great Barrington, MA: SteinerBooks, 2010).
11 Marie Savitch: *Marie Steiner-von Sivers. Mitarbeiterin Rudolf Steiners.* Dornach 1965, p. 114.

12   According to Marie Savitch Rudolf Steiner abided by his intention of 1914 until 1922. "The solemn opening of the Goetheanum with the performance of the fifth mystery drama was intended to take place at Christmas 1923/24" (Ibid., p. 130). But the plans were thwarted by the fire that destroyed the Goetheanum. The Christmas Conference was held—as a social mystery drama—at the end of 1923 and beginning of 1924. Looking back, Rudolf Steiner wrote in 1924 that he had demurred at "opening the Goetheanum personally." He added: "The program of that lecture cycle was not suitable for such a festive act which would require an event more in harmony with the original idea of the building. It never happened. The Goetheanum died away before it was possible. Those who loved it celebrate a continuous memorial in their hearts" (*Der Goetheanum-Bau inmitten der Kultur-Krisis der Gegenwart.* CW 36. Dornach 1961, pp. 329f.).

13   Rudolf Steiner gave eighteen (!) lectures during the first academic course in Dornach. (*Erster Hochschulkurs*, Sept. 27 to Oct. 16, 1920. In: Rudolf Steiner: *Grenzen der Naturerkenntnis* [English trans.: *The Boundaries of Natural Science* (CW 322). Hudson, NY: Anthroposophic Press, 1983]; *Physiologisch-Therapeutisches auf Grundlage der Geisteswissenschaft.* CW 314 ["Physiology and Therapy Based on Spiritual Science"; not available in English]; *Der Baugedanke von Dornach.* CW 288 ["The Art of Recitation and Declamation"; not available in English]; *Die Kunst der Rezitation und Deklamation.* CW 281. [English trans.: *Poetry and the Art of Speech.* London: Rudolf Steiner House, 1981]) He also presented many topics for discussion, answered questions, introduced the eurythmy performances and a youth appeal, and spoke at the opening ceremony (and the previous evening) as well as at the end of the course.

14   Cf. Rudolf Steiner: *Die befruchtende Wirkung der Anthroposophie auf die Fachwissenschaften. Zweiter anthroposophischer Hochschulkurs in Dornach* (Apr. 3–10, 1921). CW 76 ("The Fructifying Effect of Anthroposophy on Specialized Fields"; not available in English); *Die Aufgabe der Anthroposophie gegenüber Wissenschaft und Leben. Darmstaedter Hochschulkurs* (July 27–30, 1921). CW 77a ("The Task of Anthroposophy in Relation to Science and Life: The Darmstadt College Course; not available in English); *Erneuerungs-Impulse für Kultur und Wissenschaft. Berliner Hochschulkurs* (Mar. 6–11, 1922). (*Reimagining Academic Studies: Science, Philosophy, Education, Social Science, Theology, Linguistics* [CW 81]. Great Barrington, MA: SteinerBooks,

2012); *Damit der Mensch ganz Mensch werde. Die Bedeutung der Anthroposophie im Geistesleben der Gegenwart. Den Haager Hochschulkurs* (Apr. 7–12, 1922). CW 82. ("So That the Human Being Can Become Whole"; not available in English).

15 Rudolf Steiner: *Die Wirklichkeit der höheren Welten.* CW 79. Dornach 1988, p. 173 (emphasis added) ("The Reality of the Higher Worlds"; not available in English).

16 In looking back to the first academic course in Dornach, Rudolf Steiner wrote in the spring of 1924: "The first series of lectures had not grown organically from the same idea as the building itself. They were carried into the purely anthroposophical building" (*Der Goetheanum-Bau inmitten der Kultur-Krisis der Gegenwart.* CW 36, p. 328). Nine months earlier, Rudolf Steiner had spoken about his impressions of the first academic course in a members' lecture: "In 1920, the series of lectures was given that I mentioned earlier, on the initiative of the scholars who had thankfully joined the Anthroposophical Society. They organized the lectures and set up the program which they then presented to me. I firmly believe that there should be absolute freedom in the Anthroposophical Society. People outside often think everything that happens in the Anthroposophical Society must be thought out by Steiner. But most of the things that are going on here Steiner would never think of. The Anthroposophical Society is not here for me; it is here for the anthroposophists. So I sat there, giving my full attention to these lecture courses of September and October 1920—I just give a summary, it is no criticism—and I let my gaze wander along the inside of the building. In the weekly journal 'Das Goetheanum' I described, for eurythmy for instance, how the lines of the Goetheanum find continuation in the movements. That was originally meant to be the case with everything else at the Goetheanum. I let my spiritual eye wander and perceive how the—sculpted and painted—interior design harmonized with what the lecturers were saying. There was no need to point that out at the time, but I found that what was said out of Anthroposophy in the narrowest sense harmonized perfectly with the architectural style. But with a whole number of lectures one felt: they should not be given until outbuildings have been built that comply in style with these special studies and contemplations. In the ten years of its existence the Goetheanum shared the destiny of the Anthroposophical Society. That was evident from the harmony or disharmony between the architecture and the life inside it; how something inorganic entered into the stream of the anthroposophical spiritual movement" (*Anthroposophische*

Notes

    Gemeinschaftsbildung. Dornach 1989, p. 139f. (English trans.: *Awakening to Community* [CW 257]. Spring Valley, NY: Anthroposophic Press, 1974. Tr. M. Spock).

17 Rudolf Steiner: *Die Konstitution der Allgemeinen Anthroposophischen Gesellschaft und der Freien Hochschule für Geisteswissenschaft.* CW 260a, p. 278.

18 Christoph Lindenberg wrote on Rudolf Steiner's response to the first academic course: "Rudolf Steiner did not show his feelings. Toward the end of the academic course he merely asked that the satire 'The Song of Initiation,' which he had written in 1915 when the Society experienced a serious crisis, be included in the program. For anybody who knew Steiner even just slightly that should have been a sign" (Christoph Lindenberg: *Rudolf Steiner: eine Biographie. Band. 2. 1915–1925.* Stuttgart 1988, p. 723).

19 Rudolf Steiner: *Esoterische Unterweisungen für die erste Klasse der Freien Hochschule für Geisteswissenschaft am Goetheanum 1924.* CW 270a, p. 150. In the first Class Lesson he gave in Prague Rudolf Steiner also said: "We are really not interested in imitating today's universities or in achieving what they achieve in a different form. That is what people strove for when they thought that everybody should have their own view and not be influenced by me. It was tried in Dornach; it never sat well with me. But we are obliged to let things rise to the surface in this movement. Now that the trial period is over and we know that nothing can be gained by that approach, the Dornach School for Spiritual Science will cease to give the impression that it wants to compete with other universities. Instead it will offer what no ordinary education system offers and what every person must long for today" (*Esoterische Unterweisungen für die erste Klasse der Freien Hochschule für Geisteswissenschaft am Goetheanum 1924.* CW 270c, p. 160). In Bern he also spoke about the events that led to the (new) founding of the School for Spiritual Science: "The School for Spiritual Science has been through a probation period. Before I took on the chair of the Anthroposophical Society we observed repeatedly that there was an impulse to model the Goetheanum on the traditional universities. We can say today that the attempt was not successful although it was a valid and necessary effort. We have seen enough trials now, there won't be any more" (Ibid., p. 191).

20 Rudolf Steiner: *Die Konstitution der Allgemeinen Anthroposophischen Gesellschaft und der Freien Hochschule für Geisteswissenschaft.* CW 260a, p.105.

21 Rudolf Steiner: *Das Schicksalsjahr 1923 in der Geschichte der Anthroposophischen Gesellschaft.* CW 259. Dornach 1991, p. 251.
22 Ibid., p. 254 ("The Year of Destiny, 1923 in the History of the Anthroposophical Society: From the Burning of the Goetheanum to the Christmas Conference"; not available in English).
23 Just before the fire, at Christmas 1922, a science conference was held at the Goetheanum. It was not initiated by Rudolf Steiner either but he was asked for a contribution. Rudolf Steiner said to Lilly Kolisko: "People treat me as if I was their bootjack! They organize conferences without asking me and present me with a ready-made program inviting me to contribute lectures. I will have no more of that" (Lilly Kolisko: *Eugen Kolisko. Ein Lebensbild*, p. 68. Steiner nevertheless gave the lectures he was asked for; cf.: *Der Entstehungsmoment der Naturwissenschaft in der Weltgeschichte und ihre seitherige Entwickelung.* [English trans.: *The Origins of Natural Science* (CW 326). Hudson, NY: Anthroposophic Press, 1985]).Emanuel Zeylmans van Emmichoven wrote on the mood at the Goetheanum on the morning of the fire (based on unpublished notes by Oskar Schmiedel): "On Sunday, December 31, a mood of depression and confusion prevailed that was further aggravated by a morning lecture given in the White Auditorium by an employee of the Futurum Laboratory who had not applied to the conference organizers for permission to speak. According to an eyewitness, the lecture was even worse than expected. It was generally thought that the speaker was insane. His presentation was so confused and chaotic that it was impossible to make out what it was about. Rudolf Steiner, who arrived later, was shocked. The reporter met Steiner on leaving the Goetheanum. Steiner asked him, who was almost distraught, how it was possible that such a lecture was presented" (Emanuel Zeylmans van Emmichoven: *Wer war Ita Wegman. Eine Dokumentation*, vol. 1, p. 122. Available in English as *Who was Ita Wegman? A Documentation.* 3 vols. Spring Valley 1995).
24 Rudolf Steiner: *Die Konstitution der Allgemeinen Anthroposophischen Gesellschaft und der Freien Hochschule für Geisteswissenschaft.* CW 260a, p. 105.
25 During the Christmas Conference, Rudolf Steiner sharply criticized such misrepresentation of Anthroposophy (cf. Rudolf Steiner: *Die Weihnachtstagung zur Begründung der Allgemeinen Anthroposophischen Gesellschaft 1923/24.* CW 260. Dornach 1995. See also Peter Selg's description: "Die 'Intentionen der

Weihnachtstagung.' In: Peter Selg: *"Die Medizin muss Ernst machen mit dem geistigen Leben."* Rudolf Steiners Hochschulkurse für die 'jungen Mediziner.' Dornach 2006, pp. 13–22). The facts surrounding the problems the Anthroposophical Society struggled with in the years before the Christmas Conference have, to this day, not been penetrated or researched. We hardly know what Rudolf Steiner objected to so resolutely and can therefore not understand his attitude. It is equally unclear how the "diplomatic" representation of Anthroposophy that Steiner criticized could continue in spite of the Christmas Conference or recur later in slightly moderated forms. In-depth investigation and analysis of the events *before* the Christmas Conference seem essential prerequisites for gaining an understanding of Rudolf Steiner's behavior, of the change brought about by the Christmas Conference, and many of today's problems. Cf. my study "Rudolf Steiner und das zweite Goetheanum." In: *Vom Umgang mit Rudolf Steiners Werk. Ursprung, Krise und Zukunft des Dornacher Goetheanums.* Dornach 2007, pp. 21–64.

26 Cf. the discussion forums with Rudolf Steiner in: *Das Schicksalsjahr 1923 in der Geschichte der Anthroposophischen Gesellschaft.* CW 259; and the lecture cycle of June 1923: *Die Geschichte und die Bedingungen der anthroposophischen Bewegung im Verhältnis zur Anthroposophischen Gesellschaft. Eine Anregung zur Selbstbesinnung* (English trans.: *The Anthroposophic Movement.* [CW 258].Hudson, NY: Anthroposophic Press, 1993). There is plenty of evidence of Rudolf Steiner's (at least partial) despair about the state of the Anthroposophical Society, including the national societies, up to the end of 1923.

27 Rudolf Steiner: *Die Weihnachtstagung zur Begründung der Allgemeinen Anthroposophischen Gesellschaft 1923/24.* CW 260, p. 279.

28 Rudolf Steiner spoke to Ita Wegman about this, saying: "In ancient times a person might have had to pay with his sudden death for carrying out such an esoteric act. Now, *with the power of Christ*, such things are possible, and because humanity in its present state needs it, one must have the confidence and also the courage to do such powerful things." (From Sergei O. Prokofieff: *Menschen mögen es hören. Das Mysterium der Weihnachtstagung.* Stuttgart 2002, p. 7 [English trans.: *May Human Beings Hear It! The Mystery of the Christmas Conference.* London: Temple Lodge, 2004]).

29 Rudolf Steiner: *Die Weltgeschichte in anthroposophischer Beleuchtung und als Grundlage der Erkenntnis des Menschengeistes.*

Dornach 1991, p. 148. (English trans.: *World History in the Light of Anthroposophy* [CW 233]. London; Rudolf Steiner Press, 1977).

30   For the European development in the early 1920s cf. also Mark Mazower's enlightening study, *Dark Continent: Europe's Twentieth Century.* New York: Vintage, 2000.

31   Rudolf Steiner: *Die Konstitution der Allgemeinen Anthroposophischen Gesellschaft und der Freien Hochschule für Geisteswissenschaft.* CW 260a, p. 190.

32   Cf. Peter Selg: *The Figure of Christ: Rudolf Steiner and the Spiritual Intention behind the Goetheanum's Central Work of Art.* London: Temple Lodge, 2009.

33   Rudolf Steiner: *Esoterische Unterweisungen für die erste Klasse der Freien Hochschule für Geisteswissenschaft am Goetheanum 1924.* CW 270c, p. 14.

34   On the spiritual history of the foundation of the Anthroposophical Society, see Sergei O. Prokofieff's study: *Die Geburt der christlichen Esoterik im 20. Jahrhundert und die ihr widerstrebenden okkulten Mächte.* Dornach 1997.

35   Rudolf Steiner: *Die Konstitution der Allgemeinen Anthroposophischen Gesellschaft und der Freien Hochschule für Geisteswissenschaft.* CW 260a, p. 172; emphasis added.

36   September 20, 1913. In: Michael Bauer: *Gesammelte Werke. Band 5. Briefe* (ed. Christoph Rau). Stuttgart 1997, pp. 40f.

37   Rudolf Steiner: *Mysterienstätten des Mittelalters.* CW 233a. Dornach 1991, pp. 134f.

38   Rudolf Steiner: *Esoterische Unterweisungen für die erste Klasse der Freien Hochschule für Geisteswissenschaft am Goetheanum 1924.* CW 270b, p. 31; emphasis added.

39   Rudolf Steiner: *Die Weihnachtstagung zur Begründung der Allgemeinen Anthroposophischen Gesellschaft 1923/24.* CW 260, pp. 275f.

40   Rudolf Steiner: *Die Konstitution der Allgemeinen Anthroposophischen Gesellschaft und der Freien Hochschule für Geisteswissenschaft.* CW 260a, p. 100.

41   Rudolf Steiner: *Esoterische Unterweisungen für die erste Klasse der Freien Hochschule für Geisteswissenschaft am Goetheanum 1924.* CW 270c, p. 12; emphasis added.

42   Rudolf Steiner: *Esoterische Unterweisungen für die erste Klasse der Freien Hochschule für Geisteswissenschaft am Goetheanum 1924.* CW 270c, p. 191.

43 Rudolf Steiner: *Die Konstitution der Allgemeinen Anthroposophischen Gesellschaft und der Freien Hochschule für Geisteswissenschaft.* CW 260a, p. 358.

44 Ibid., p. 101.

45 Rudolf Steiner: *Esoterische Unterweisungen für die erste Klasse der Freien Hochschule für Geisteswissenschaft am Goetheanum 1924.* CW 270c, p. 159.

46 Rudolf Steiner: *Die Weltgeschichte in anthroposophischer Beleuchtung und als Grundlage der Erkenntnis des Menschengeistes.* p. 118. (English trans.: *World History and the Mysteries: In the Light of Anthroposophy* [CW 233]. London: Rudolf Steiner Press, 1997).

47 On the origin and background of these courses cf. Peter Selg: *Helene von Grunelius und Rudolf Steiners Kurse für junge Mediziner. Eine Studie.* Dornach 2003.

48 Cf. Rudolf Steiner: *Meditative Betrachtungen und Anleitungen zur Vertiefung der Heilkunst.* CW 316; and Peter Selg: "*Die Medizin muss Ernst machen mit dem geistigen Leben. Rudolf Steiners Hochschulkurse für die 'jungen Mediziner.'*" Dornach 2006.

49 "It seems important that immediately after arriving in Dornach [in April 1924] we received our certificates as members of the First Class of the School for Spiritual Science, even those who had not applied yet" (Madeleine P. van Deventer: *Die anthroposophisch-medizinische Bewegung in den verschiedenen Etappen ihrer Entwicklung.* Arlesheim 1992, p. 28. For the difficult situation the group of young doctors and medical students found themselves in at the time, see Peter Selg: *Die Briefkorrespondenz der "jungen Mediziner." Eine dokumentarische Studie zur Rezeption von Rudolf Steiners "Jungmediziner-Kursen."* Dornach 2005, pp. 65ff.). The (mostly very young) priests of the Christian Community were also admitted as a group to the School for Spiritual Science in 1924, although some of them—like some of the young physicians—were not members of the Anthroposophical Society (cf. Wolfgang Gädeke: *Anthroposophie und die Fortbildung der Religion.* Flensburg 1990, p. 390). For the faculty of teachers of the Stuttgart Waldorf School, see note 16. For Rudolf Steiner's usual handling of membership applications for the First Class, see note 219, and Sergei O. Prokofieff/Peter Selg: *Die Weihnachtstagung und die Begründung der neuen Mysterien.* Arlesheim 2011, pp. 93ff.

50 Rudolf Steiner: *Esoterische Unterweisungen für die erste Klasse der Freien Hochschule für Geisteswissenschaft am Goetheanum 1924.* CW 270a, p. 149.

51 Rudolf Steiner: *Esoterische Unterweisungen für die erste Klasse der Freien Hochschule für Geisteswissenschaft am Goetheanum 1924.* CW 270c, p. 162.

52 Rudolf Steiner: *Meditative Betrachtungen und Anleitungen zur Vertiefung der Heilkunst.* CW 316. Dornach 2003, p. 137; emphasis added ("Meditative Views and Guidance for Deepening the Art of Healing"; unavailable in English).

53 This is why the individual Sections were established. Some of them have now taken up their work; and we have, most importantly, begun with the General Anthroposophical Section in Dornach: the section that is there for all who seek to deepen their soul life. (Rudolf Steiner: *Esoterische Unterweisungen für die erste Klasse der Freien Hochschule für Geisteswissenschaft am Goetheanum 1924.* CW 270c, p. 192).

54 Rudolf Steiner talked in Torquay about the medical research he was conducting with Ita Wegman. Cf. Rudolf Steiner: *Das Initiatenbewusstsein* (English trans.: *True and False Paths in Spiritual Investigation* [CW 243]. Hudson, NY: Anthroposophic Press, 1985); and Emanuel Zeylmans van Emmichoven: "Hintergründe der anthroposophischen Heilkunst," in: *Wer war Ita Wegman. Eine Dokumentation.* Band 2, pp. 99–117.

55 Cf. Peter Selg: "Zur Entstehungsgeschichte des Buches 'Grundlegendes für eine Erweiterung der Heilkunst nach geisteswissenschaftlichen Erkenntnissen.'" In: Peter Selg (ed.): *"Und in der Tat, dies wirkte." Die Krankengeschichten des Buches "Grundlegendes für eine Erweiterung der Heilkunst nach geisteswissenschaftlichen Erkenntnissen" von Rudolf Steiner und Ita Wegman. Eine Dokumentation.* Dornach 2007, pp. 13–23.

56 Rudolf Steiner saw the meetings and case studies he had with the practicing physicians from Dec. 31, 1923 to Jan. 2, 1924 and from Apr. 21–23, 1924, as part of the tuition offered by the Medical Section (cf. Rudolf Steiner: *Physiologisch-Therapeutisches auf Grundlage der Geisteswissenschaft.* [CW 314]; "Physiology and Therapy Based on Spiritual Science"; not available in English). In early March, Steiner wrote in the *Newssheet,* under the title "The School for Spiritual Science," about the first meeting (and the first Course for Young Doctors): "The first seminar of the School for Spiritual Science took place during and immediately after the Christmas Conference. It was initiated by the Section that is led

by Ita Wegman, MD, and had two parts. During the final days of the Christmas Conference the practicing physicians who attended as members of the society met and collected questions that I then based our discussions on. The leadership of the School for Spiritual Science will try to find ways of continuing what was started there. Written information will be sent out as soon as possible on what can be arranged in that respect. After the Christmas Conference the same section offered a course for young physicians and medical students that addressed the soul life of the practicing physician. The course was offered to meet the spiritual needs expressed by medical students who had come to the Goetheanum. It was meant as an introduction to the knowledge of the world and human beings that physicians need to have and aimed to reveal the sources from which true medical ethos, the 'medical spirit,' arises. Owing to limited time, only guidelines and indications could be given. But we hope what has been started will be continued in the spirit described" (Rudolf Steiner: *Die Konstitution der Allgemeinen Anthroposophischen Gesellschaft und der Freien Hochschule für Geisteswissenschaft.* CW 260a, pp. 165f.). All the specialist courses given at the Goetheanum in 1924 were organized by the School for Spiritual Science or its Sections. The courses for young physicians and medical students stood out, owing to their esoteric dimension and mantric structure. They were the only meetings that showed clearly how Rudolf Steiner intended to develop the work of the Esoteric School of the Goetheanum in the various fields.

57 "I asked: 'Would it not be possible to found a medical mystery school?' Rudolf Steiner's answer: 'That is not so easy. It must be wanted by the spiritual world and it needs people who want to receive it.' After some days a positive response from the Mercury–Raphael spirit; his task of renewing ancient ritual that was solemnly celebrated in a sacred place, under the guidance of Mercury–Raphael. Mine the task to seek spirit-imbued human souls who understand such rituals and are willing to hear Raphael's words" (Ita Wegman's notebook; Ita Wegman Archives).

58 Cf. Peter Selg: *Die Briefkorrespondenz der "jungen Mediziner". Eine dokumentarische Studie zur Rezeption von Rudolf Steiners "Jungmediziner"-Kursen,* pp. 145ff. For the wording of the pledge cf. Rudolf Steiner: *Mantrische Sprüche. Seelenübungen II. 1903–1925* (CW 268). Dornach 1999, p. 309. ("Soul Exercises. vol. 2: Mantric Verses, 1903–1925"; not available in English).

59 Rudolf Steiner: *Esoterische Unterweisungen für die erste Klasse der Freien Hochschule für Geisteswissenschaft am Goetheanum 1924.* CW 270c, p. 12.
60 Ibid., p. 192.

Chapter 2

1 Rudolf Steiner: *Esoterische Unterweisungen für die erste Klasse der Freien Hochschule für Geisteswissenschaft am Goetheanum 1924.* CW 270a, p. 124.
2 Rudolf Steiner: *Esoterische Unterweisungen für die erste Klasse der Freien Hochschule für Geisteswissenschaft am Goetheanum 1924.* CW 270c, p. 12.
3 Ibid., p. 161.
4 Ibid., p. 123.
5 Rudolf Steiner: *Esoterische Unterweisungen für die erste Klasse der Freien Hochschule für Geisteswissenschaft am Goetheanum 1924.* CW 270a, p. 81.
6 Ibid., p. 129.
7 Ibid., p. 149.
8 Ibid., p. 145.
9 Ibid., p. 124.
10 Ibid., p. 149.
11 Rudolf Steiner: *Esoterische Unterweisungen für die erste Klasse der Freien Hochschule für Geisteswissenschaft am Goetheanum 1924.* CW 270c, p. 161.
12 Rudolf Steiner: *Bausteine zu einer Erkenntnis des Mysteriums von Golgatha.* CW 175. Dornach 1996, pp. 33f.
13 Rudolf Steiner: *Esoterische Unterweisungen für die erste Klasse der Freien Hochschule für Geisteswissenschaft am Goetheanum 1924.* CW 270c, p. 161.
14 Rudolf Steiner: *Esoterische Unterweisungen für die erste Klasse der Freien Hochschule für Geisteswissenschaft am Goetheanum 1924.* CW 270b, p. 124.
15 Rudolf Steiner: *Esoterische Unterweisungen für die erste Klasse der Freien Hochschule für Geisteswissenschaft am Goetheanum 1924.* CW 270c, p. 123.
16 Ibid., p. 80.
17 Ibid., p. 89.
18 Ibid., p. 14.
19 Ibid.
20 Ibid., p. 45.

21 Cf. in particular Rudolf Steiner: *Esoterische Betrachtungen karmischer Zusammenhänge*, vols. 3–6. CWs 237–240.
22 Rudolf Steiner: *Anthroposophische Leitsätze*. Dornach 1998, p. 59ff. (English trans.: *Anthroposophical Leading Thoughts: Anthroposophy as a Path of Knowledge: The Michael Mystery* [CW 26]. London: Rudolf Steiner Press, 1998.
23 Rudolf Steiner: *Esoterische Unterweisungen für die erste Klasse der Freien Hochschule für Geisteswissenschaft am Goetheanum 1924*. CW 270b, p. 158.
24 Rudolf Steiner: *Esoterische Unterweisungen für die erste Klasse der Freien Hochschule für Geisteswissenschaft am Goetheanum 1924*. CW 270a, p. 124.
25 Rudolf Steiner: *Esoterische Unterweisungen für die erste Klasse der Freien Hochschule für Geisteswissenschaft am Goetheanum 1924*. CW 270b, p. 115.
26 Rudolf Steiner: *Esoterische Unterweisungen für die erste Klasse der Freien Hochschule für Geisteswissenschaft am Goetheanum 1924*. CW 270c, p. 161.
27 Ibid., p. 45.
28 Ibid., p. 80.
29 Ibid., p. 89.
30 Ibid., p. 99.
31 Ibid., p. 188.
32 Ibid. p. 80.
33 On the task of "interpreting" the light cf. Hella Wiesberger: "It had become a cultural-historical task to explain these new revelations that have appeared, especially since Kali Yuga ended in 1899, to humanity and to understand through them the greatest mystery of humanity, the Mystery of Golgotha. Rudolf Steiner took on this task, pointing out that 'if Anthroposophy is not understood in that way it is not understood at all'" *(Rudolf Steiners esoterische Lehrtätigkeit*, p. 18).
34 Rudolf Steiner: *Esoterische Unterweisungen für die erste Klasse der Freien Hochschule für Geisteswissenschaft am Goetheanum 1924*. CW 270a, p. 124.
35 Rudolf Steiner: *Esoterische Unterweisungen für die erste Klasse der Freien Hochschule für Geisteswissenschaft am Goetheanum 1924*. CW 270c, p. 102.
36 Cf. also Sergei O. Prokofieff: *Die Grundsteinmeditation. Ein Schlüssel zu den neuen christlichen Mysterien*. Dornach 2003, pp. 67ff. (English trans.: *The Foundation Stone Meditation. A Key to the Christian Mysteries*. London: Temple Lodge, 2006).

37 Rudolf Steiner: *Esoterische Unterweisungen für die erste Klasse der Freien Hochschule für Geisteswissenschaft am Goetheanum 1924.* CW 270c, p. 124.
38 Rudolf Steiner: *Esoterische Unterweisungen für die erste Klasse der Freien Hochschule für Geisteswissenschaft am Goetheanum 1924.* CW 270b, p. 174.
39 Rudolf Steiner: *Esoterische Unterweisungen für die erste Klasse der Freien Hochschule für Geisteswissenschaft am Goetheanum 1924.* CW 270a, p. 124.
40 Rudolf Steiner: *Die Konstitution der Allgemeinen Anthroposophischen Gesellschaft und der Freien Hochschule für Geisteswissenschaft.* CW 260a, p. 109.
41 Rudolf Steiner: *Esoterische Unterweisungen für die erste Klasse der Freien Hochschule für Geisteswissenschaft am Goetheanum 1924.* CW 270c, p. 119.
42 Rudolf Steiner: *Die Konstitution der Allgemeinen Anthroposophischen Gesellschaft und der Freien Hochschule für Geisteswissenschaft.* CW 260a, p. 124.
43 Rudolf Steiner: *Esoterische Unterweisungen für die erste Klasse der Freien Hochschule für Geisteswissenschaft am Goetheanum 1924.* CW 270a, p. 16.
44 Rudolf Steiner: *Esoterische Unterweisungen für die erste Klasse der Freien Hochschule für Geisteswissenschaft am Goetheanum 1924.* CW 270b, p. 11.
45 Cf. also Rudolf Steiner's writings: *How to Know Higher Worlds* (CW 10). Hudson, NY: Anthroposophic Press, 1994; *An Outline of Esoteric Science* (CW 13). Hudson, NY: Anthroposophic Press, 1997; *A Way of Self-Knowledge: And the Threshold of the Spiritual World* (CW 16/17) Great Barrington, MA: SteinerBooks, 2006.
46 Rudolf Steiner: *Esoterische Unterweisungen für die erste Klasse der Freien Hochschule für Geisteswissenschaft am Goetheanum 1924.* CW 270a, p. 124.
47 Rudolf Steiner described the central substance of the First Class in greatest detail when he wrote to the members of the General Anthroposophical Society: "The lectures given now to the General Anthroposophical Section of the School for Spiritual Science offer a preliminary view of the 'threshold' experienced between the world of the senses and the suprasensory world. Those who truly seek to know what is essentially human must understand that all the beauty, magnificence and sublimity revealed by 'nature' will not lead us to the human essence. Our inner self, even though it is active in the outside world, does *not* originate in the natural but

in the spiritual world. Neither our senses nor our brain-bound reason are able to penetrate into the spiritual world. Both must cease to be active before we can confront the world of our origin. When their activity ends we are at first unable to perceive anything. We look around and see only darkness that appears as a 'void'. This inability will yield to the faculties of spiritual vision if we are aware of higher forces within us that form 'spiritual senses' just as the physical forces in our organism form the bodily senses. Such development relies on the total transformation of our inner essence from one form of existence into another. As this transformation proceeds it is important that we do not lose the one form of existence before we gain the other. The right transformation process depends on the right 'threshold' experience. True self-knowledge is only possible from beyond the threshold. If we want to receive communication, with our ordinary consciousness, of insights gained by someone beyond the threshold, we must have an idea of what happens at the threshold. Only if we know of the conditions that are necessary to gain suprasensory knowledge will we be able to understand that knowledge in the right way.—We will not be able to give content to the words spoken out of suprasensory vision until we understand what the seeing person went through before gaining the power to speak such words. If that is not the case we will be under the impression that these suprasensory words are ordinary words of the sensory world and they will confuse us. The words become treacherous and lead to illusion rather than knowledge.—These indications are intended as an initial characterization of the esoteric effect of the School for Spiritual Science" (Rudolf Steiner: *Die Konstitution der Allgemeinen Anthroposophischen Gesellschaft und der Freien Hochschule für Geisteswissenschaft.* CW 260a, pp. 201f.).

48 Rudolf Steiner: *Esoterische Unterweisungen für die erste Klasse der Freien Hochschule für Geisteswissenschaft am Goetheanum 1924.* CW 270a, p. 103.

49 Peter Selg: "*Die Medizin muss Ernst machen mit dem geistigen Leben.*" *Rudolf Steiners Hochschulkurse für die "jungen Mediziner.*" pp. 55ff.

50 Rudolf Steiner: *Esoterische Unterweisungen für die erste Klasse der Freien Hochschule für Geisteswissenschaft am Goetheanum 1924.* CW 270b, p. 82.

51 Ibid., p. 151.

52 Ibid., p. 156.

53 Ibid., p. 58f.

54 Ibid., pp. 157f.
55 Ibid., p. 159.
56 Rudolf Steiner: *Esoterische Unterweisungen für die erste Klasse der Freien Hochschule für Geisteswissenschaft am Goetheanum 1924.* CW 270a, p. 128.
57 Ibid., p. 129.
58 Starting with the second Class Lesson, Rudolf Steiner spoke about this repeatedly most resolutely. He also broached the subject with Ita Wegman, who wrote: "This [Christmas Conference] apparently met with great enthusiasm. But did people really take it to heart? The calling on the elementary spirits as witnesses in the Foundation Stone Meditation, requesting that human beings may hear it, failed to achieve its objective. Human ears remained deaf and the elementary spirits waited for what could come from human beings, but Dr. Steiner told me that they grew restless when the response remained too weak. He then spoke of a promise he had made to the spiritual world that he would have to keep if there was no change" (Ita Wegman: "Notes for a lecture about Rudolf Steiner, London, Feb. 27, 1931"). Ita Wegman Archives, Arlesheim, Switzerland. Cf. Emanuel Zeylmans van Emmichoven: *Wer war Ita Wegman. Eine Dokumentation*, vol. 1. p. 315. Friedrich Rittelmeyer remembered a conversation he had with Rudolf Steiner in May 1924: "He seemed almost shattered by the failure of his followers" (*Meine Lebensbegegnung mit Rudolf Steiner.* Stuttgart 1983, pp. 156f.).
59 Rudolf Steiner: *Die Konstitution der Allgemeinen Anthroposophischen Gesellschaft und der Freien Hochschule für Geisteswissenschaft.* CW 260a, p. 137.
60 Rudolf Steiner: *Esoterische Unterweisungen für die erste Klasse der Freien Hochschule für Geisteswissenschaft am Goetheanum 1924.* CW 270c, p. 125; emphasis added.
61 Cf. also Hella Wiesberger: "Rudolf Steiners Wirken und das fünfte der sieben grossen Geheimnisse des Lebens," in: *Rudolf Steiners esoterische Lehrtätigkeit* (Dornach 1997, pp. 90ff). Hella Wiesberger concluded her considerations with the words: "Especially since the outbreak of World War I, Steiner spoke ever more emphatically and in ever more detail of the workings of evil, particularly in history, as aberrations from the progressing stream of evolution. The great importance attached to the knowledge of evil as a fundamental mystery of our age explains why the Goetheanum building, as the visible symbol of the anthroposophic movement, was being associated with it. When

the foundation stone was laid Steiner honored an 'occult obligation' and spoke for the first time of the Fifth Gospel, the Gospel of Knowledge, that was built around the macrocosmic Lord's Prayer: 'The Evils hold sway /Witness of "I"-hood freeing itself / selfhood-guilt through others begotten / Experienced in the daily bread /Wherein the Heavens' will does not hold sway, For man turned away from your kingdom / And forgot your names /You Fathers in the Heavens.' In the ten years of intensive building work that followed, the central motif, the sculptural group of 'The Representative of Humanity between Lucifer and Ahriman' was created with the help of many volunteers. The sculpture was a visible expression of the dual nature of the fifth mystery of life. 'The Representative of Humanity'—Christ as recognized by Rudolf Steiner, as the master of masters—represents the full analogy of microcosm and macrocosm. Through the love that emanates from him, he overcomes Lucifer and Ahriman, the powers of aberration and evil. When the building was destroyed by fire just before its completion in the New Year's night of 1922, the wood sculpture was the only part that survived: legacy of and memorial to its creator providing insight into the deepest mysteries of life in our fifth era" (ibid., pp. 95f.). Cf. also Peter Selg: *The Figure of Christ. Rudolf Steiner and the Spiritual Intention Behind the Goetheanum's Central Work of Art.* London: Temple Lodge, 2008.

62 Rudolf Steiner: *Esoterische Unterweisungen für die erste Klasse der Freien Hochschule für Geisteswissenschaft am Goetheanum 1924.* CW 270a, p. 81.
63 Ibid., p. 128.
64 Ibid., p. 151.
65 Ibid., p. 131.
66 Rudolf Steiner: *Esoterische Unterweisungen für die erste Klasse der Freien Hochschule für Geisteswissenschaft am Goetheanum 1924.* CW 270b, p. 176.
67 Rudolf Steiner: *Esoterische Unterweisungen für die erste Klasse der Freien Hochschule für Geisteswissenschaft am Goetheanum 1924.* CW 270a, p. 129.

CHAPTER 3

1 Wolfgang Moldenhauer: Letter to Kurt Franz David of Nov. 15, 1972. Quoted from Johannes Kiersch: *A History of the School for Spiritual Science. The First Class*, p. 31.

2 Quoted from Thomas Meyer: *Ludwig Polzer-Hoditz. Ein Europäer.* Basel 1994, p. 565.
3 Cf. Peter Selg: *"Ich bleibe bei Ihnen." Rudolf Steiner und Ita Wegman. München, Pfingsten 1907. Dornach 1923–1925.* Stuttgart 2007, pp. 56ff.
4 Rudolf Steiner: *Esoterische Unterweisungen für die erste Klasse der Freien Hochschule am Goetheanum 1924.* CW 270a, p. 149.
5 Rudolf Steiner: *Esoterische Unterweisungen für die erste Klasse der Freien Hochschule am Goetheanum 1924.* CW 270c, p. 161.
6 Cf. Rudolf Steiner: *From the History and Contents of the First Section of the Esoteric School, 1904–1914* (CW 264). Great Barrington, MA: SteinerBooks, 2010; *"Freemasonry" and Ritual Work: The Misraim Service: Texts and Documents from the Cognitive-Ritual Section of the Esoteric School 1904-1919* (CW 265). Great Barrington, MA: SteinerBooks, 2007; *Esoteric Lessons*, CW 266, vols. 1–3, Great Barrington, MA: SteinerBooks, 2007–2011; and Hella Wiesberger: *Rudolf Steiners esoterische Lehrtätigkeit. Wahrhaftigkeit-Kontinuität-Neugestaltung.* Dornach 1997.
7 Emanuel Zeylmans worked up until his death on an annotated edition of Rudolf Steiner's entire notes for Ita Wegman. His in-depth studies were published in 2009 by the Ita Wegman Institute from his estate: *Die Erkraftung des Herzens. Eine Mysterienschulung der Gegenwart. Rudolf Steiners Zusammenarbeit mit Ita Wegman.*
8 Cf. Ita Wegman's letter to Rudolf Steiner of November 1906, in: Peter Selg: *"Ich bin für Fortschreiten." Ita Wegman und die Medizinische Sektion.* Dornach 2002, p. 20 (English trans.: *I Am for Going Ahead: Ita Wegman's Work for the Social Ideals of Anthroposophy*, Great Barrington, MA: SteinerBooks, 2012).
9 To Mathilde Scholl. In: Rudolf Steiner: *Zur Geschichte und aus den Inhalten der ersten Abteilung der Esoterischen Schule 1904–1914.* CW 264. Dornach 1984, pp. 44f. (*From the History and Contents of the First Section of the Esoteric School, 1904–1914*).
10 Ibid., p. 58.
11 Cf. Hella Wiesberger: *Rudolf Steiners esoterische Lehrtätigkeit*, p. 141. ("This union of disciples who were faithfully devoted to the Masters and HPB [Helena Petrovna Blavatsky] was under her sole leadership and wholly independent of the exoteric [Theosophical] society if one disregards the fact that only members of the T.S. [Theosophical Society] were admitted to it." Ibid.)

Notes

12   Ibid., pp. 73ff.; cf. the memories of members who took part in the early esoteric lessons, cited by Hella Wiesberger, describing Rudolf Steiner's attitude and appearance (ibid., p. 121).

13   "The Esoteric School had been secret under Blavatsky. You only knew of its existence if you were personally invited to attend." (Editor's prefatory comment to: Rudolf Steiner: *Esoterische Unterweisungen für die erste Klasse der Freien Hochschule am Goetheanum 1924.* CW 270a, p. ix.)

14   On July 19, 1924 Rudolf Steiner spoke in Arnhem about the connection between the cosmic Michael events (in the cosmic "Michael School") and the origin of Goethe's Tale: "Up in the spiritual world powerful cosmic images were prepared for the intelligent but truly spiritual creation that was to manifest as Anthroposophy. Elements of this filtered through and made a certain impression on Goethe. It reached him in miniature images, as it were. Goethe was unaware of the great, powerful images that were prepared up high. He worked the miniatures into his *Tale of the Green Snake and the Beautiful Lily.*' A wonderful projection!... It was a first reflection of the mighty imaginations that appeared in in the spiritual world in the early nineteenth and even late eighteenth century. (Rudolf Steiner: *Esoterische Betrachtungen karmischer Zusammenhänge.* Vol. 6. Dornach 1992, p. 178 [English trans.: Karmic Relationships: Esoteric Studies, vol. 6 (CW 240). London: Rudolf Steiner Press, 2006]).

15   "In *this* lecture [Sept. 29, 1900], I became entirely esoteric after Goethe's Tale. It was a crucial experience to be able to speak in words that came from the spirit world, after I had been restricted by circumstances, during my time in Berlin, to let the spiritual reality only shine through in my presentations" (Rudolf Steiner: *Mein Lebensgang.* Dornach 2000, pp. 391ff. [English trans.: *Autobiography: Chapters in the Course of My Life, 1861–1907* (CW 28). Great Barrington, MA: SteinerBooks, 2006]).

16   Hella Wiesberger: *Rudolf Steiners esoterische Lehrtätigkeit,* p. 306.

17   Entry in Ita Wegman's note book, 1933. Ita Wegman Archives.

18   Rudolf Steiner: *Aus den Inhalten der esoterischen Stunden. Band 1: 1904–1909.* Dornach 1995, p. 542. (English trans.: *Esoteric Lessons, 1904–1909: From the Esoteric School,* vol. 1 [CW 266/1]. Great Barrington, MA: SteinerBooks, 2007).

19   For details cf. Peter Selg: *"Ich bleibe bei Ihnen." Rudolf Steiner und Ita Wegman. München, Pfingsten 1907. Dornach 1923–1925,* pp. 13ff.

20   Ibid.

21 Cf. Hella Wiesberger: *Rudolf Steiners esoterische Lehrtätigkeit*, pp. 133ff.
22 "Documents de Barr," in: Rudolf Steiner/Marie Steiner-von Sivers: *Briefwechsel und Dokumente 1901–1925*. Dornach 2002, p. 26. (English trans.: Correspondence and Documents 1901–1925 [CW 262]. Hudson, NY: Anthroposophic Press, 1988).
23 Rudolf Steiner: *Zur Geschichte und aus den Inhalten der ersten Abteilung der Esoterischen Schule 1904 bis 1914*. CW 264, p. 329.
24 Entry in Ita Wegman's note book, 1933. Ita Wegman Archives.
25 Rudolf Steiner: *Aus den Inhalten der esoterischen Stunden. Band I: 1904–1909.* p. 258. (English trans.: *Esoteric Lessons 1913–1923: From the Esoteric School*, vol. 3 [CW 266/1]. Great Barrington, MA: SteinerBooks, 2011).
26 Rudolf Steiner: *Aus den Inhalten der esoterischen Stunden. Band 3: 1913–14/ 1920–1923*. CW 266/3, p. 264. Correction of Rudolf Steiner's handwritten note for Ita Wegman (cf. p. 67).
27 Ibid., p. 265.
28 Ibid., p. 268.
29 When Rudolf Steiner was asked, in a faculty meeting at the Stuttgart Steiner School toward the end of 1921, whether he would go on with the esoteric lessons, he said that esotericism had been a "painful chapter" in the book of the anthroposophical movement and Society. ("That is very difficult to do. Until now, I have always had to avoid them. As you know, I gave a number of such studies years ago, but I had to stop because people misused them. Esotericism was simply taken out into the world and distorted. In that regard, nothing in our esoteric movement has ever been as damaging as that. All other esoteric study, even in less than honorable situations, was held intimately. That was the practice over a long period of time. Cliques have become part of the Anthroposophical Society and they have set themselves above everything else, unfortunately, also above what is esoteric. Members do not put the anthroposophical movement as such to the fore, but, instead, continually subject it to the interests of cliques. The anthroposophical movement is dividing into a number of factions.... Esotericism is a painful chapter in the book of the anthroposophical movement." *Faculty Meetings with Rudolf Steiner*, vol. 1 (CW 300). Hudson, NY: Anthroposophic Press, 1998, p. 305. On Rudolf Steiner's individual esoteric lessons between 1918 and 1923 and his insistence on quality if there should be a new start, cf. Hella Wiesberger: "Von den neuen Ansätzen esoterischer Lehrtätigkeit nach dem Ersten Weltkrieg," in: *Rudolf Steiners esoterische Lehrtätigkeit*, pp. 297–307.

30 Cf. Rudolf Steiner: *Die Anthroposophie und ihre Gegner.* CW 255b. Dornach 2003 ("Anthroposophy and Its Opponents, 1919–1921"; unavailable in English).
31 Cf. Emanuel Zeylmans van Emmichoven: *Who was Ita Wegman? A documentation*, vol. 1. Spring Valley 1995. Tr. D. Winter.
32 Rudolf Steiner: *Die soziale Grundforderung unserer Zeit–In geänderter Zeitlage.* Dornach 1990, p. 122. (English trans.: *The Challenge of the Times* [CW 186]. Spring Valley, NY: Anthroposophic Press, 1941).
33 Cf. Rudolf Steiner's letter to Ita Wegman from Koberwitz, written on June 11, 1924, in: Emanuel Zeylmans van Emmichoven: *Wer war Ita Wegman. Eine Dokumentation*, vol. 1. pp. 206ff; and in: Peter Selg: *"Ich bleibe bei Ihnen." Rudolf Steiner und Ita Wegman. München, Pfingsten 1907.* Dornach 1923–1925, pp. 77ff. (facsimile and transcription).
34 Ibid.
35 Ita Wegman Archives. First published in: Emanuel Zeylmans van Emmichoven: *Wer war Ita Wegman. Eine Dokumentation*, vol. 1. p. 241.
36 For details cf. Peter Selg: *"Ich bleibe bei Ihnen." Rudolf Steiner und Ita Wegman. München, Pfingsten 1907.* Dornach 1923–1925, pp. 57ff.
37 Emanuel Zeylmans van Emmichoven: *Wer war Ita Wegman. Eine Dokumentation*, vol. 1. pp. 128ff.
38 Rudolf Steiner: Letter to Edith Maryon of Aug. 23, 1923. In: *Rudolf Steiner/Edith Maryon: Briefwechsel (1912–1924).* CW 263/1. Dornach 1990, p. 143.
39 Rudolf Steiner: *Iniations-Erkenntnis.* CW 227. Dornach 1982, p. 159 ("The Mission of the New Spiritual Revelation: The Christ Event as the Central Event of the Ground of Evolution"; unavailable in English).
40 Ita Wegman: *An die Freunde.* Arlesheim 1986, p. 154.
41 Emanuel Zeylmans van Emmichoven: *Wer war Ita Wegman. Eine Dokumentation*, vol. 1. p. 206
42 On Ita Wegman's "individuality," cf. Peter Selg: *"Ich bin für Fortschreiten." Ita Wegman und die Medizinische Sektion*, pp. 79 and 88f. (*I Am for Going Ahead: Ita Wegman's Work for the Social Ideals of Anthroposophy*).
43 Ludwig Count Polzer-Hoditz: Dornach address of Apr. 14, 1935, quoted from: Emanuel Zeylmans van Emmichoven: *Wer war Ita Wegman. Eine Dokumentation*, vol. 3. p. 335.
44 Ibid.

45 According to Polzer-Hoditz, Rudolf Steiner spoke the central mantra of the First Class, "O man, know yourself," at the beginning of the Vienna class lesson on Sept. 30, 1923 ("personal communication," Dec. 1, 1935. Quoted from Johannes Kiersch: *A History of the School for Spiritual Science: The First Class.* p. 234).
46 Cf. note 167.
47 Ita Wegman: Notebook entry, Apr. 1925. Ita Wegman Archives. For facsimile publication of the full entry see Emanuel Zeylmans van Emmichoven: *Wer war Ita Wegman. Eine Dokumentation,* vol. 1. pp. 318ff.
48 Rudolf Steiner: *Die Konstitution der Allgemeinen Anthroposophischen Gesellschaft und der Freien Hochschule für Geisteswissenschaft.* CW 260a, p. 371.
49 Cf. Rudolf Steiner: *Die Weltgeschichte in Anthroposophischer Beleuchtung.* CW 233. Dornach 1991).
50 Cf. in particular Rudolf Steiner's lecture of December 30, 1923 (ibid., p. 115ff.) According to a letter Ita Wegman wrote to Otto Palmer on Dec. 18, 1923, Rudolf Steiner's original intention was to devote the final Christmas Conference lectures to medicine ("After consultation with Dr. Steiner, the Doctor will devote the lectures on the last three days of the Christmas Conference to general medical topics, for all members." Ita Wegman Archives). Steiner's lecture of Dec. 31 was strongly colored, however, by memories of the fire that had destroyed the First Goetheanum a year earlier. In his concluding lecture of Jan.1, 1924, Steiner spoke about the main spiritual task of the newly founded School for Spiritual Science.
51 On Sept. 28, 1935, six months after Rudolf Steiner's death, Ita Wegman wrote to Toni Völker: "*When the Doctor founded the Michael School, he appointed me as his assistant*" (Ita Wegman Archives). The fact that she saw assisting—as a helper, in the words of Polzer-Hoditz—as her particular task also impacted on her work in the Medical Section. There is no doubt that, for Ita Wegman, Rudolf Steiner was the true "leader" of that section of the School for Spiritual Science. On July 16, 1924, she wrote in answer to the letter from a fellow physician who pronounced himself astonished at the fact that such a responsible task was entrusted to a "lady" (since he was "not much in favor of ladies in leading positions"): "I appreciate your truthful admission that you find it difficult to relate to the Medical Section that has now been established because it is, as you say, led by a 'lady.' I do not intend to work very publicly and my work in the Section will consist in my closer collaboration with the Doctor and in carrying out what the Doctor deems necessary to

achieve an extension of medicine through spiritual science" (In: Ita Wegman: *Medizinisch-therapeutische Korrespondenzen.* Ed. Peter Selg. Dornach 2007, p. 86).

52 Cf. Emanuel Zeylmans van Emmichoven: *Wer war Ita Wegman. Eine Dokumentation*, vol. 1. pp. 166f.

53 On Rudolf Steiner's situation after the Goetheanum was destroyed by flames, cf. the witness reports in Peter Selg: *Marie Steiner-von Sivers. Aufbau und Zukunft des Werkes von Rudolf Steiner.* Dornach 2006, pp. 195ff.

54 Ita Wegman Archives. First published in: Emanuel Zeylmans van Emmichoven: *Wer war Ita Wegman. Eine Dokumentation,* vol. 1. pp. 241f. For a facsimile print of Rudolf Steiner's handwritten verse, see Peter Selg: *"Ich bleibe bei Ihnen." Rudolf Steiner und Ita Wegman. München, Pfingsten 1907. Dornach 1923–1925.* p. 68.

55 Rudolf Steiner: *Die Weihnachtstagung zur Begründung der Allgemeinen Anthroposophischen Gesellschaft 1923/24.* CW 260, p. 222.

56 Ibid., p. 143ff.; cf. Peter Selg: *Vom Umgang mit Rudolf Steiners Werk. Ursprung, Krise und Zukunft des Dornacher Goetheanum,* pp. 112ff.

57 Cf. Emanuel Zeylmans van Emmichoven: *Wer war Ita Wegman. Eine Dokumentation*, vol. 2. pp. 99–117.

58 Ita Wegman's note book (1935). Ita Wegman Archives. For a facsimile reproduction of the entry, see Peter Selg: *Geistiger Widerstand und Überwindung. Ita Wegman 1933–1935.* Dornach 2005, p. 176.

59 On Rudolf Steiner's personal way of dealing with requests for admission to the School for Spiritual Science cf. the remarkable chapter "Die Bearbeitung der Aufnahme-Anträge für die Erste Klasse durch Rudolf Steiner," in: Kurt Franz David: "Die Einrichtung der Ersten Klasse durch Rudolf Steiner und deren Schicksale bis zur Gegenwart" (pp. 30–34). David wrote: "Rudolf Steiner examined all applications himself, from Jan. 1924 until his death. Requests addressed to Dr. Wegman were passed on to him. His way of dealing with them remained the same throughout the fourteen to fifteen months. He usually wrote his comments by hand in the top left hand corner. In most cases he wrote "yes RS," occasionally "no RS" or "wait RS." If he did not know a member well enough he would make inquiries.—This did not change when he became ill. At the beginning, when he still expected to recover soon, he often withheld a decision until he had opportunity

to speak to the person in question" (ibid., p. 31. Goetheanum Archives). Despite his conclusion that Rudolf Steiner rejected only "few" applications, David showed in his documentation impressively how precise and differentiated Rudolf Steiner's handling of the applications was, right up to his death.

David documented, for instance, the following details: "On application letters we find comments such as the following in Rudolf Steiner's handwriting: 'too early' (letter from Hamburg, Apr. 25, 1924); 'wait until I've seen her again!' (letter from Stuttgart, Apr. 30, 1924); 'wait till she comes again' (letter from Basel, May 2, 1924); 'yes, yes of course' (letter from Bonn, May 10, 1924); 'wait till November' (letter from Sonnenberg, May 14, 1924); 'must wait!' (letter from Stuttgart, June 20, 1924); 'needs to wait for personal introduction' (letter from Stuttgart, Sept. 8, 1924); 'should wait a while! 3 months maybe St.' (letter from Stuttgart, Nov. 18, 1924); 'should wait and reapply in about 4 months' (letter from Stuttgart, Sept. 20, 1924); 'should wait a while, maybe 4 months, maybe I can meet him first R St.' (letter from Stuttgart, Nov. 19, 1924); 'No! One needs to write and tell him that he has to wait a while' (letter from Grafenstaden, Nov. 24, 1924); 'needs to wait a bit, has hardly been a member for a year—maybe the time can be reduced later, but not yet R St' (letter from Jena, Dec. 8, 1924); 'must wait half a year RS' (letter from Cannstadt, Dec. 10, 1924). With applicants who had not been members for two years yet, Rudolf Steiner usually insisted on waiting: 'one needs to ask when membership began and with what branch R St' (letter from Stuttgart, Nov. 19, 1924); 'must wait till two years have passed R St' (letter from Stuttgart, Nov. 23, 1924); 'needs to be asked when membership began and in what branch R St' (letter from Stuttgart, Nov. 27, 1924).

Often he [Rudolf Steiner] referred to a particular person as a source for more information: 'ask Rittelmeyer' (letter from Göttingen of Sep. 27, 1924); 'ask the council in Königsberg RS' (letter from Königsberg of Oct. 2, 1924); 'can be done only by Mlle Sauerwein RS' (letter from Paris of Oct. 19, 1924); 'ask Rietmann in St. Gallen! R S' (letter from St. Gallen of Nov. 14, 1924); 'ask at the clinic in Stuttgart' (letter from Seiffersdorf of Jan. 6, 1925).

The following is a selection of further comments: 'careful with this. No' (Letter from Zurich, May 4, 1924); 'a sentimental but very good person. Yes' (letter from Lehrte, May 1924); letter from Tübingen, May 4, 1924 with lengthy descriptions of how the applicant brought spiritual-scientific knowledge about the metals to his employees: 'yes, the rest is nonsense;' letter from Stuttgart, Oct. 28, 1924, indicating a visit to Dornach at Christmas: 'yes, but point out that there will be little, if anything, at Christmas R St'....'needs to wait until he can approach the matter more calmly' (letter from Stuttgart, Dec. 2, 1924); 'I cannot possibly work my way through such concoctions' (letter from Stuttgart, Dec. 2, 1924, consisting of 9 typed pages)" (Kurt Franz David: "Die Einrichtung der Ersten Klasse durch Rudolf Steiner und deren Schicksale bis zur Gegenwart," pp. 32–34. Goetheanum Archives).

60 Ita Wegman: Letter to Albert Steffen, Mar. 16, 1926. Ita Wegman Archives. The letter was first published in total in: Emanuel Zeylmans van Emmichoven: *Wer war Ita Wegman. Eine Dokumentation*, vol. 3. pp. 65ff.

61 Ibid., p. 67

62 Ita Wegman Archives. Facsimile reproduction in Peter Selg: *"Ich bleibe bei Ihnen." Rudolf Steiner und Ita Wegman. München, Pfingsten 1907. Dornach 1923–1925*, p. 85.

63 Ita Wegman: Letter to Albert Steffen, Aug. 21, 1925. Ita Wegman Archives. Letter first published in its full length in: Emanuel Zeylmans van Emmichoven: *Wer war Ita Wegman. Eine Dokumentation*, vol. 3. pp. 58f.

64 Ibid., p. 59.

Chapter 4

1 Ita Wegman Archives, Arlesheim.
2 Ibid.
3 Goetheanum Archives.
4 Cf. CW 270, vol. 3.
5 Ita Wegman's letter to Albert Steffen of March 16, 1926. Ita Wegman Archives, Arlesheim.
6 Goetheanum Archives. Quoted from Johannes Kiersch: *Zur Entwicklung der Freien Hochschule für Geisteswissenschaft. Die Erste Klasse.* Dornach 2005, p. 51 (English trans.: *A History of the School for Spiritual Science: The First Class*. London: Temple Lodge, 2006).
7 Lecture draft Mar. 1935. Ita Wegman Archives. Facsimile in Peter Selg: *Geistiger Widerstand und Überwindung. Ita Wegman 1933–1935*. Dornach 2005, p. 176.
8 Protokoll, p. 256. Goetheanum Archives.

9   Cf. J. Emanuel Zeylmans van Emmichoven: *Die Erkraftung des Herzens. Eine Mysterienschule der Gegenwart. Rudolf Steiners Zusammenarbeit mit Ita Wegman.* Arlesheim 2009.
10 Ibid., p. 177.
11 Emanuel Zeylmans van Emmichoven (who died on July 9, 2008) had been unaware of Ita Wegman's statement of Nov. 19, 1930 (that she possessed a written document about the ritual act that preceded the handing over of the rose cross and the admittance as joint leader of the Michael School). I only came across the statement myself after his death, during my own research into Elisabeth Vreede (2009) in the Goetheanum Archives. Emanuel Zeylmans did not address the question whether the description of the ritual preceding the handing over of the rose cross was among Ita Wegman's esoteric documents. He published the text as part of his collection titled "The Great Rose Cross Mediation," but remained uncertain about its content and its time of origin. ("It is unfortunately not possible to date this important exercise. In the context of the other exercises I would assume that it goes back to the fall of 1923" [*Die Erkraftung des Herzens. Eine Mysterienschule der Gegenwart. Rudolf Steiners Zusammenarbeit mit Ita Wegman.* p. 177].)
12 Cf. the exercises in Rudolf Steiner's and Ita Wegman's handwriting, pages 71–76.
13 Cf. Ita Wegman's numeration on page 76 and Emanuel Zeylman van Emmichoven's corresponding comments in *Die Erkraftung des Herzens*, p. 175.
14 English translation from: Rudolf Steiner, *Breathing the Spirit: Meditations for Times of Day and Seasons of the Year.* London: Rudolf Steiner Press, 2007. p. 64.
15 Ibid.
16 Ibid., p. 333.
17 Ibid., pp. 404ff.

Chapter 5

1   Ita Wegman: Letters to George Kaufmann, June 19, 1935. Ita Wegman Archives.
2   Ita Wegman: Letter to Albert Steffen, Aug. 21, 1925. Ibid. In: Emanuel Zeylmans van Emmichoven: *Wer war Ita Wegman. Eine Dokumentation*, vol. 3. p. 59.
3   Cf. Johannes Kiersch: *A History of the School for Spiritual Science. The First Class*, pp. 38ff.

Notes

4   Reproduction of essays from the *Members' Newsletter* [*Nachrichtenblatt*] in: Ita Wegman: *An die Freunde*. Arlesheim 1986.
5   *Members' Newsletter,* June 14, 1925.
6   Ibid., Aug. 16, 1925.
7   Ibid.
8   Ibid.
9   "Dr. Wegman's repeated efforts (initially in conversation with Marie Steiner but especially in the council meetings in Rudolf Steiner's studio in the first weeks following his passing away) to resume the reading of the class lessons failed at first due to Marie Steiner's resistance. Marie Steiner suggested to wait a year and examine one's maturity. Her attitude as well as her proposal to authorize Mrs. Kolisko with the reading made the conflicting views apparent that she and Dr. Wegman held about the continuation of the First Class. Dr. Wegman felt a special connection with the class due to her earlier close collaboration with Rudolf Steiner. She saw it as her given task, a view that was not shared by Marie Steiner" (Kurt Franz David: "Die Einrichtung der ersten Klasse durch Rudolf Steiner und deren Schicksale bis zur Gegenwart," p. 11).
10 *Newsletter,* Aug. 16, 1925.
11 Ita Wegman: *Letter to Mien Viehoff.* Oct. 24, 1939. Ita Wegman Archives.
12 Ita Wegman: Letter to Maria Röschl, Feb. 22, 1935. Ita Wegman Archives.
13 Ita Wegman: Introductory words before a class lesson, see ch. 6
14 Ita Wegman: Letter to Albert Steffen, Mar. 16, 1926. Ita Wegman Archives. In: Emanuel Zeylmans van Emmichoven: *Wer war Ita Wegman. Eine Dokumentation*, vol. 3, pp. 66f.
15 Ita Wegman: Introductory words before a class lesson, see ch. 6.
16 Cf. Rudolf Steiner: *Die Konstitution der Allgemeinen Anthroposophischen Gesellschaft und der Freien Hochschule für Geisteswissenschaft.* CW 160a, p. 186. ("With esoteric contents the question is whether or not people possess the necessary understanding of the heart.") Rudolf Steiner described his positive impressions when holding two class lessons in Prague (on April 3 and 5, 1924): "It was deeply satisfying for me to see the souls that I had often seen before me at events in Prague. In many eyes I saw a deep sense of being one with the anthroposophical life substance. I was aware of many receptive hearts. Such hearts are essential for the cultivation of esoteric life. Because the intellect is powerless unless power streams to it from the heart. Such understanding from the heart

is no less 'logical' than that of the head. But it is not seen as logical in ordinary life because there, it does not need to unfold the inner power of suprasensory 'logic.' In ordinary life the mind is responsible for logic and the heart can go about its own business, untouched by logic because it can be corrected by the mind. People are usually afraid of a 'heart logic' because they fear that the heart might lose its warmth when logic enters it. But people only have that fear until they realize how much warmth the soul experiences when it comprehends spiritual ideas. People who don't feel that warmth do no *live* in the ideas of the spirit. They only *think* ideas that have died in the soul; ideas that they hear expressed in words into which an initiate once poured his living spiritual experiences" (ibid., pp. 198f.). Rudolf Steiner agreed to the class lessons he had given in Prague that had been taken down in shorthand being read out verbatim in two-week intervals (cf. Johannes Kiersch: *A History of the School for Spiritual Science. The First Class*, p. 120). The exceptional situation might have arisen due to the special way Rudolf Steiner's lessons were received in Prague and due to his special relationship with the work there.

17   On the evening when Edith Maryon crossed the threshold Rudolf Steiner began the class lesson by saying emphatically: "It may suffice to say today that the First Class has lost a truly devoted pupil. Miss Maryon was prominent among the pupils who devote the greatest diligence and deep inner feeling to the First Class. Although she was severely ill she partook in our esoteric work and allowed the exercises given to her to work in her by living with them most intimately" (Rudolf Steiner: *Esoterische Unterweisungen für die erste Klasse der Freien Hochschule für Geisteswissenschaft am Goetheanum 1924*. CW 270b, p. 29; emphasis added).

18   Ita Wegman: introduction to a class lesson, see chapter 6.

19   Ibid.

20   Cf. Emanuel Zeylmans van Emmichoven: *Wer war Ita Wegman. Eine Dokumentation*. vol. 2; Peter Selg: "Ita Wegman und die Heilpädagogen," in: *"Ich bin für Fortschreiten." Ita Wegman und die Medizinische Sektion*. Dornach 2002, pp. 67–111. Peter Selg: *Der Engel über dem Lauenstein. Siegfried Pickert, Ita Wegman und die Heilpädagogik*. Dornach 2004.

21   Ita Wegman Archives.

22   Cf. Peter Selg: *Geistiger Widerstand und Überwindung. Ita Wegman 1933–1935*, pp. 29ff.

23   Quoted from Peter Selg: *Rudolf Steiner—zur Gestalt eines geistigen Lehrers. Eine Einführung*. Dornach 2007, p. 71 (English

trans.: *Rudolf Steiner as a Spiritual Teacher: From Recollections of Those Who Knew Him*. Great Barrington, MA: SteinerBooks, 2010).

24 Quoted from Peter Selg: *Geistiger Widerstand und Überwindung. Ita Wegman 1933–1935*, pp. 76ff.

25 Ibid., pp. 84f.

26 Ita Wegman: Letter to Maria Röschl, Feb. 22, 1935. Ita Wegman Archives.

27 For Ita Wegman's journey to Palestine in the fall of 1934 cf. Peter Selg: *Geistiger Widerstand und Überwindung. Ita Wegman 1933–1935*, pp. 110–153. For Rudolf Steiner's lectures on the Fifth Gospel cf. Rudolf Steiner: *Aus der Akasha Chronik. Das Fünfte Evangelium* (English trans.: *The Fifth Gospel: From the Akashic Record* [CW 148]. London: Rudolf Steiner Press, 1998); and Peter Selg: *Rudolf Steiner und das Fünfte Evangelium. Eine Studie*. Dornach 2005 (English trans.: *Rudolf Steiner and the Fifth Gospel: Insights into a New Understanding of the Christ Mystery*. Great Barrington, MA: SteinerBooks, 2010).

28 For the Mystery of "evil"—as the fifth of the seven "great mysteries of life"—and its relationship to the Christ statue in Dornach cf. Hella Wiesberger: "Rudolf Steiners Wirken und das fünfte der sieben großen Geheimnisse des Lebens," in: Hella Wiesberger: *Rudolf Steiners esoterische Lehrtätigkeit*. pp. 90–96. Cf. note 154.

29 The letter was first published in: Peter Selg: *Geistiger Widerstand und Überwindung. Ita Wegman 1933–1935*. pp. 199–202.

30 Willem Zeylmans van Emmichoven: Letter to George Kaufmann, December 13, 1934. Quoted from Johannes Kiersch: *A History of the School for Spiritual Science. The First Class*, p. 143.

31 Ita Wegman: Letter to Walter Johannes Stein, Jan. 9, 1935. Ita Wegman Archives.

32 Ita Wegman: Letter to Alice Wengraf, Jan. 31, 1935. Ita Wegman Archives.

33 Ita Wegman: Letter to Klara Župič-Dajčeva, Feb. 1, 1935. Ita Wegman Archives.

34 Ita Wegman: Letter to Gertrud Goyert, Jan. 29, 1935. Ita Wegman Archives.

35 Ita Wegman: Letter to George Kaufmann, June 19, 1935. Ita Wegman Archives.

36 Ibid.

37 Werner Pache: Diary entry, transcript in Ita Wegman Archives.

38 There is no indication in any of Ita Wegman's letters or notes to suggest that she considered moving away from Rudolf Steiner's

class texts or changing to "free" lessons. All the passages in her letters of 1934/35 that refer to the First Class speak of her wish to detach the lessons from the conflicts of the Anthroposophical Society. That was also the reason why they were removed from official events of the Society. Early in 1935 Ita Wegman for the first time refused to travel to the annual general meeting of the British society, which was led by D.N. Dunlop, and hold the class lessons there (although the members there were supportive of her.) Cf. Peter Selg: *Geistiger Widerstand und Überwindung. Ita Wegman 1933–1935*, pp. 158ff.

39 Conversation with the author. Arlesheim, Apr. 3, 2008.

40 Cf. p. 93 in the text.—For many years Ita Wegman was coached by speech therapist Martha Hemsoth (1887–1936), cf. Emanuel Zeylmans van Emmichoven: *Wer war Ita Wegman. Eine Dokumentation*, vol. 2. pp. 76f.

41 Rudolf Steiner spoke of the "occult act" of the class lesson "in which the verses are received" in the third repeat lesson on September 11, 1924 in Dornach. Cf. Rudolf Steiner: *Esoterische Unterweisungen für die erste Klasse der Freien Hochschule für Geisteswissenschaft am Goetheanum 1924*. CW 270c, p. 63.

42 "If any of it fell into the wrong hands it would lose its effect on those who receive it for its effect. If the mantric verses or *the content of what is presented here* were to be passed on to the wrong people, they would lose their effect on those who are sitting here." (Ibid., p. 103; emphasis added)

43 Ibid., pp. 124f.

44 "And you will have the right impression if you take every word spoken within this school as being spoken because the speaker feels responsible toward none but the spiritual powers that guide the anthroposophical movement" (Ibid., p. 161).

45 Rudolf Steiner: *Esoterische Betrachtungen karmischer Zusammenhänge. Zweiter Band*. Dornach 1988, p. 254 (English trans.: *Karmic Relationships: Esoteric Studies*, vol. 2 [CW 236]. London: Rudolf Steiner Press, 1997).

46 Cf. Rudolf Steiner: *Anthroposophische Leitsätze*. CW 26. Dornach 1998, pp. 97f.

47 Ita Wegman wrote a remarkable (and singular) letter on September 9, 1925, in response to Zeylmans' questions concerning his task as conveyor of the class mantras in Holland: "I meant that you recite the mantras like a meditation that is spoken out loud. When you have spoken the mantras, end with the Michael sign and the words 'E D N, I C M, P S S R.' Then close with the

words: 'We end with the sign of Michael' and give the sign. When you have said this and given the sign you translate the words as indicated: I love the father.... At the end give the sign again while speaking the words in Latin. I do not want to say much in between or talk about it because I intend to initiate a ritual. Therefore: speak the mantas out loud, give the Michael sign. That's it. If that seems too short seeing that all the [class] members are gathered together, wait a moment, then read something by Rudolf Steiner or say something yourself, ideally about Michael. For me it is important that the explanations that need to be given for all these esoteric things stream through me out of what Dr. Steiner has given. I believe that much good will come from this institution and hope for your goodwill, collaboration and support" (Ita Wegman Archives). In my view Zeylmans' membership in the esoteric core of the Medical Section needs to be seen in relation with Ita Wegman's intention to establish a cult.

48 Ita Wegman: Letter to Marianne Bischof, Dec. 12, 1940. Ita Wegman Archives.
49 Ita Wegman: Letter to Madeleine van Deventer, Jan. 20, 1941. Ibid.
50 Liane Collot d'Herbois: "Erinnerungen an Ita Wegman." *Ita Wegman-Fonds für soziale und therapeutische Hilfstätigkeiten.* 1993, p. 40.
51 Rudolf Steiner: *Esoterische Unterweisungen für die erste Klasse der Freien Hochschule für Geisteswissenschaft am Goetheanum 1924.* CW 270a, p. 124.
52 Rudolf Steiner: *Anthroposophische Menschenerkenntnis und Medizin.* Dornach 1994, p. 220. (English trans.: *The Healing Process: Spirit, Nature & Our Bodies* [CW 319]. Great Barrington, MA: SteinerBooks, 2010).
53 Ita Wegman Archives.

Chapter 6

1 Ita Wegman Archives.

Appendix

1 Faculty Meetings with Rudolf Steiner, vol. 2, CW 300c, p. 701.
2 Ibid.
3 Ibid., p. 704
4 Ibid., pp. 705f.
5 Lilly Kolisko: *Eugen Kolisko. Ein Lebensbild.* Gerabronn-Crailsheim, p. 90.

6   Rudolf Steiner to Lilly Kolisko. In: Lilly Kolisko: Letter to Ita Wegman of Nov. 2, 1924. Ita Wegman Archives.
7   Cf. Rudolf Steiner: *Die Methodik des Lehrens und die Lebensbedingungen des Erziehens.* CW 308, p. 93.
8   Unpublished. Ita Wegman Archives, Arlesheim.
9   Cf. Peter Selg: *Helene von Grunelius und Rudolf Steiners Kurse für die jungen Mediziner. Eine biographische Studie,* Dornach 2003.
10 Cf. Peter Selg: *"Die Medizin muss Ernst machen mit dem geistigen Leben." Rudolf Steiners Hochschulkurse für die "jungen Mediziner."* Dornach 2006.
11 Madeleine P. van Deventer: *Die anthroposophisch-medizinische Bewegung in den verschiedenen Etappen ihrer Entwicklung.* Arlesheim 1982, p. 28.
12 Rudolf Steiner: *Esoterische Unterweisungen für die erste Klasse der Freien Hochschule für Geisteswissenschaft am Goetheanum 1924.* CW 270a, p. 149.
13 Rudolf Steiner: *Esoterische Unterweisungen für die erste Klasse der Freien Hochschule für Geisteswissenschaft am Goetheanum 1924.* CW 270c, p. 162.
14 Rudolf Steiner: *Meditative Betrachtungen und Anleitungen zur Vertiefung der Heilkunst.* CW 316, p. 223. ("Meditative Views and Guidance for Deepening the Art of Healing"; unavailable in English).
15 Ibid., pp. 73f.
16 Ibid., p. 137.
17 On the "esoteric center of the Medical Section," its origin and goals cf. Rudolf Steiner: *Das Zusammenwirken von Ärzten und Seelsorgern.* CW 318, pp. 165f.; and Peter Selg: *Die Briefkorrespondenz der "jungen Mediziner." Eine dokumentarische Studie zur Rezeption von Rudolf Steiners "Jungmediziner"-Kursen.* Dornach 2005, pp. 145ff.
18 Gottfried Husemann: 'Die Begründung der Christengemeinschaft.' In: Erika Beltle, Kurt Vierl (eds): *Erinnerungen an Rudolf Steiner.* Stuttgart 1979, p. 311.
19 *Faculty Meetings with Rudolf Steiner,* vol. 2. CW 300c, p. 771.
20 Rudolf Steiner: *Vorträge und Kurse über christlich-religiöses Wirken,* V. CW 346, p. 44.
21 Rudolf Steiner: *Mysterienstätten des Mittelalters. Rosenkreuzertum und modernes Einweihungsprinzip.* CW 233a, pp. 134f. ("Mystery Sites of the Middle Ages: Rosicrucianism and the Principle of Modern Initiation: Easter as a Part of the History of the Mysteries of Humanity"; unavailable in English); cf. also Sergei

O. Prokofieff's fundamental study: *Die Erste Klasse der Michael-Schule und ihre christologischen Grundlagen.* Dornach 2009. ("The First Cass of the Michael School and Its Christological Basis"; unavailable in English).

22 Rudolf Steiner: *Meditative Betrachtungen und Anleitungen zur Vertiefung der Heilkunst.* CW 316, p. 220 (English trans.: *The Course for Young Doctors*, Spring Valley, NY: Mercury Press, 1997).

23 Rudolf Steiner: *Esoterische Unterweisungen für die erste Klasse der Freien Hochschule für Geisteswissenschaft am Goetheanum 1924.* CW 270a, p. 151.

Books in English Translation by Peter Selg

ON RUDOLF STEINER:

Rudolf Steiner and Christian Rosenkreutz (2012)

Rudolf Steiner as a Spiritual Teacher: From Recollections of Those Who Knew Him (2010)

ON CHRISTOLOGY:

The Creative Power of Anthroposophical Christology: An Outline of Occult Science · The First Goetheanum · The Fifth Gospel · The Christmas Conference (with Sergei O. Prokofieff) (2012)

Christ and the Disciples: The Destiny of an Inner Community (2012)

The Figure of Christ: Rudolf Steiner and the Spiritual Intention behind the Goetheanum's Central Work of Art (2009)

Rudolf Steiner and the Fifth Gospel: Insights into a New Understanding of the Christ Mystery

Seeing Christ in Sickness and Healing (2005)

ON GENERAL ANTHROPOSOPHY:

The Agriculture Course, Koberwitz, Whitsun 1924: Rudolf Steiner and the Beginnings of Biodynamics (2010)

The Culture of Selflessness: Rudolf Steiner, the Fifth Gospel, and the Time of Extremes (2012)

The Fundamental Social Law: Rudolf Steiner on the Work of the Individual and the Spirit of Community (2011)

Karl König's Path to Anthroposophy (2008)

The Mystery of the Heart: The Sacramental Physiology of the Heart in Aristotle, Thomas Aquinas, and Rudolf Steiner (2012)

The Path of the Soul after Death: The Community of the Living and the Dead as Witnessed by Rudolf Steiner in his Eulogies and Farewell Addresses (2011)

Rudolf Steiner and the School for Spiritual Science: The Foundation of the "First Class" (2012)

Rudolf Steiner's Intentions for the Anthroposophical Society: The Executive Council, the School for Spiritual Science, and the Sections (2011)

ON ANTHROPOSOPHICAL MEDICINE AND CURATIVE EDUCATION:

The Child with Special Needs: Letters and Essays on Curative Education (Ed.) (2009)

I Am for Going Ahead: Ita Wegman's Work for the Social Ideals of Anthroposophy (2012)

Ita Wegman and Karl König: Letters and Documents Karl König's Path to Anthroposophy (2009)

Karl König: My Task: Autobiography and Biographies (Ed.) (2008)

ON CHILD DEVELOPMENT AND WALDORF EDUCATION:

The Essence of Waldorf Education (2010)

A Grand Metamorphosis: Contributions to the Spiritual-Scientific Anthropology and Education of Adolescents (2008)

I Am Different from You: How Children Experience Themselves and the World in the Middle of Childhood (2011)

The Therapeutic Eye: How Rudolf Steiner Observed Children (2008)

Unbornness: Human Pre-existence and the Journey toward Birth (2010)

Ita Wegman Institute
for Basic Research into Anthroposophy

Pfeffinger Weg 1 a CH 4144 Arlesheim, Switzerland
www.wegmaninstitute.ch
e-mail: sekretariat@wegmaninstitute.ch

The Ita Wegman Institute for Basic Research into Anthroposophy is a non-profit research and teaching organization. It undertakes basic research into the lifework of Dr. Rudolf Steiner (1861–1925) and the application of Anthroposophy in specific areas of life, especially medicine, education, and curative education. Work carried out by the Institute is supported by a number of foundations and organizations and an international group of friends and supporters. The Director of the Institute is Prof. Dr. Peter Selg.

www.ingramcontent.com/pod-product-compliance
Lightning Source LLC
Chambersburg PA
CBHW020932090426
42736CB00010B/1111